Delemere

Harappa
Mohenjo-daro

Baalbek

Sandawe

nbabwe

# THE PAST
# IS HUMAN

Peter White

# THE PAST
# IS HUMAN

TAPLINGER PUBLISHING COMPANY · NEW YORK

First published in the United States in 1976 by
TAPLINGER PUBLISHING CO., INC.
New York, New York

Library of Congress Catalog Card Number: LC   75-21680
ISBN 0-8008-6265-1

# A personal note

Many people have always wanted to be archaeologists and they are quite right, it's a deal of fun for much of the time. It's also very easy for us professionals to ignore those who weren't lucky enough to make it, and to write books aimed mostly at each other. I have tried to write this book for the people who don't know the technical jargon and who don't want to know it, but who have lots of questions about books like *Chariots of the Gods*. My answers to these questions are mostly second-hand, drawing on the careful study of many other archaeologists, but leaving out all their cautious "maybes" in order to bring out a story we can all appreciate.

Several people have helped me in various ways and I should like to thank especially Lesley Maynard, Jim Specht, John Clegg, John Poiner, and the various audiences who listened politely and then asked penetrating questions when I talked about these subjects. Richard Walsh and Bob Debus actually pushed me into making a book out of random thoughts. I intended to finish writing before Marcus was born, but Marilyn produced quicker than I could, so she has had to live with two pregnancies in a year. If she can still bear it this is her book.

PETER WHITE
*9th April 1973*

# Contents

# Illustrations

*between pages 112 and 113*

The stone with twelve corners, Cuzco, Peru

>M. K. Jessup, "Stone Masonry at Cuzco",
*American Anthropologist*, 1934

Bosses left on stones so that the Incas could lever them

>J. Steward (ed.), *Handbook of the South American Indians*,
American Museum of Natural History.

A rubbing of the tomb lid at Palenque

>M. Greene and J. E. S. Thompson, *Ancient Maya Relief
Sculpture*, Museum of Primitive Art, New York.

The Great Enclosure at Zimbabwe

>B. Fagan, *Southern Africa during the Iron Age*, Thames
and Hudson. Photo by D. Attenborough.

Erecting an Easter Island statue: the actual experiment

>T. Heyerdahl and E. N. Ferdon (eds.), *Archaeology of
Easter Island*, School of American Research and Museum
of New Mexico, Allen and Unwin. Photos by E. J. Scherven.

The quotation on pp. 118-19 is reprinted with the permission
of Professor R. F. Heizer and the Society for American
Archaeology.

# Figures

## MAP

# Introduction

Twentieth-century cities are alike all over the world—a vast sea of suburbs surrounding a business heart. In that smog-shrouded centre, narrow streets are lined with glass-fronted offices all set square on the street, not wasting an inch of valuable space.

But in each city there is at least one building or construction that is outstanding. In Sydney, Australia, a gigantic building whose white sails gleam in the sun juts out into the harbour; in London, England, an enormous tower provides space for hundreds of visitors who come to travel to the top of it and gaze out towards the horizon; in New York, U.S.A., people gaze towards the horizon from the head of a lady holding a torch; in Rio de Janeiro, Brazil, it is the statue of a man who towers over the city from the vantage of the highest mountain.

We know, of course, who built the Sydney Opera House, the G.P.O. tower, the Statue of Liberty, the statue of Jesus and similar edifices. But let us suppose that visitors from another planet or archaeologists from A.D. 2973 are trying to explain them. What would *they* make of their unusual features? Would they see each building as a temple perhaps, or some other strange, out-of-place relic of the past, or of another race, or of the visits of astronauts?

We might laugh at such misunderstandings as these. But there are many aspects of the past that are open to the same kind of confusion, in which we can easily attribute strange and mysterious purposes to what are, in fact, simple, straightforward objects.

This book is about some of these objects from the past. It is based on the knowledge that man's beginnings are no longer shrouded in mystery. We do not have to see man's history in terms of strange purposes and other-worldly visitors. We can explain it in terms of man's own actions and evolution.

This knowledge we derive from archaeology and similar studies. In the last twenty years it is archaeologists who have proved that man has been alive for at least two and a half million years, that he was responsible for the cave art of France 10,000 to 25,000 years ago, and that about 10,000 years ago he invented the agriculture on which we still depend. It is the archaeologists who proved Homer and Beowulf were not simply stories by finding Troy and Sutton Hoo; it was they who finally proved that the Vikings discovered America in about A.D. 1000. Archaeology is wide open to new ideas, new theories about the past. Theories, not guesses.

Archaeology is like a detective story. We may believe the butler did it, but can we prove it? Where is the mud on his boots, who saw him on the stairs at 9.23 p.m. precisely, are we quite certain that only he had access to the key to the room? We accept these standards of proof in a detective story, in court, in everyday life. Archaeologists demand similar standards of proof about the past.

Sometimes such proof is unobtainable at present. The research has not been done, or it was done a long time ago and not very well, or we are asking a question which the techniques available simply cannot answer. In such cases we make do with the most likely explanation of the facts we have.

If we want to say that much of our past was created by visitors from other worlds, we need two things—proof that man *could not* have made some of the archaeological remains we find, and *direct evidence* that astronauts did so.

This book is about some of the mysteries of man's past.

Were the things that puzzle us created by extra-terrestrial beings?

I argue that men are more creative than some of us will admit. In each case we look at, we can show that ancient men were able to carve statues, build pyramids and move mountains. They did so and we can show when and how they did so.

I also demonstrate that ancient maps are not based on satellite photographs, that astronauts did not have their portraits painted by primitive man, and that accounts of superhuman feats by flying gods are about as trustworthy as little Billy's story of the great big bully who stole his report card on the way home from school.

Where the evidence is available, the mysterious past turns out to be less strange and unexplained than you think. Men, not astronauts, created our past.

# 1. Loving Junk

Garbage, trash, litter, rubbish and junk are all part of man's way of life. Wherever we go, we expect to find junk left by the people there before us. This may be as ordinary as the beer-cans and orange-peel left by a previous camper, as unusual as the scientific instruments an astronaut left on the moon, or as beautiful as the golden tomb of the Pharaoh Tutankhamun in Egypt. But in each case what we find is essentially junk—things left by their owners who either had no intention of recovering or recycling them or who never got around to doing so. Junk is the archaeologist's paradise.

Most junk from the past, of course, is just that—old tins and pots, bones of animals that were eaten, disused roads, foundations of old buildings, ghost towns. Golden tombs and temples are rare. But the everyday garbage everyman leaves behind him—including his own skeleton—is informative because there is so much of it. From it we can reconstruct something of the lives of ordinary people, not only of priests and kings.

The basic theory behind all archaeology is pretty simple, and it comes from looking at the world around us. It is this: different people leave different sorts of garbage. You and your next-door neighbour probably live in similar houses, wear similar clothes, eat similar (but not quite the same!) food, so the stuff you throw away over the years will almost certainly be pretty similar, too—the same sorts of beer bottles, old shoes, T-bones and broken plates. If you move to a different part of the same town your garbage will probably alter—you will throw out slightly different food tins, and perhaps more whisky bottles than before because your income is higher. Move across a national border and the differences will be even more marked. The same principles apply to the differences between what is found in our cities and in villages in New Guinea or Africa.

Junk also changes over time. Today our junk includes large quantities of motor-cars and plastic bottles; our grand-parents threw away horse bones, buggy wheels and broken pottery instead. Similar kinds of changes occur in all communities.

Any archaeologist, whether dealing with Greek temples or Australian Aboriginal spearheads, is first of all concerned with detecting the similarities and differences in everyone's garbage and with understanding the reasons behind the changes. Is a change due to new inventions or warfare or differences in wealth or changes in fashion? Do two communities differ because they live in different places, or speak two dialects or practise two religions? To set up standards to judge such things by, archaeologists ask these sorts of questions about present-day or historically known communities. Two simple examples will illustrate the point.

Jim Deetz is an archaeologist with extensive experience in North America. One of the sites he worked on in southern California was a mission at La Purisima which was established by Spanish Franciscan fathers about four hundred years ago. At this mission American Indian men were given work of a kind they had never known before. One of the crafts they learnt was tanning hides to make leather, and Deetz excavated two old tanning vats at the mission. At the bottom of these vats he found a number of distinctive bone tools. They were bone scrapers, technically known as beamers, used for removing the hair from lime-soaked cow hides before they were put into a tanning solution. In shape and style these beamers are not like those used by Spaniards at the same time but are similar to bone scrapers found on American Indian camp-sites excavated near by:

their form is native in origin. But these beamers were made of cattle ribs, and cattle, of course, were introduced into California by the Spanish missionaries. So that although other bones and metal knives were available, the Indians preferred to make tools similar to those they had made before, that is, in bone, even though they were made from different animals and were being used for an entirely new purpose. The significance of this study by Deetz is that we can understand better how changes in technology occur: there was not a complete replacement of traditional arte-facts by introduced ones, but a blend between the two. By studying a number of changes of this kind some aspects of our archaeological data become clearer. We can decide, for example, whether we are dealing with a full-scale invasion, with the arrival of a new and better technology, or with simple trade between equal groups of people.

The other example comes from Mexico where George M. Foster has collected data on the pottery currently used by the villagers of Tzintzuntzan, in Mexico. Tzintzuntzan is a peasant community and their pottery is made both for home use and trade over a wide area. Foster's census of pottery used by four households showed that there was a very wide variety of forms and sizes of pots in use at any one time, for cooking, eating and storage.

It also showed how many pots of each kind were likely to be found in each house, and he was able to get some idea of how frequently pots were broken. Cooking pots, naturally enough, were broken more often than storage pots. Broken pottery is about the commonest material in most archaeological sites dated within the last six thousand years, and once we have a fair amount of information like that collected by Foster (for example, how many pots a family owns and how many they break a year) we can use it to assess such things as how long a site was occupied, how many people lived there, and even what they used their pots for. We can also begin to assess the meaning of differences in the numbers of pots at village sites—which might simply be that more food was stored at one village than at another.

We must have answers to such questions as, "How many people?" and, "How long did they live there?" before we can give a useful answer to such questions as, "Were there enough people around to build this pyramid, or carve those monuments?"

As well as observing how changes occur in present-day societies and how these would affect the garbage people leave, archaeologists also carry out experiments by setting up artificial situations and seeing what results come from them. These experiments provide principles on which to base our ideas about the past. Experiments can cover a variety of situations from seeing how many shellfish people eat at an average meal to hiring Hawaiians to paddle traditional canoes round Waikiki harbour to see how fast they go, but here another example will be used as illustration.

One of the commonest features of the English country-side are the earthworks, particularly forts made of earth banks and ditches, burial mounds of earth, artificial hills and similar constructions. The same sorts of buildings occur in America and in New Zealand, where the Maoris frequently fortified hilltops with earthen walls and terracing. How long does it take people to build these objects, using only traditional tools such as picks made of deer antlers and shovels made of the shoulder-blades of horses? The only way to find out is by experiment, so in 1960 a team of volunteers cut a ditch and built the soil into a bank at Overton Down in England. They found that modern picks and shovels were three to four times more efficient than ancient ones, with the main difference being in the shovel —shoulder-blades are just not very good for shovelling. But more importantly they found that on an average a man working with ancient tools could move about 260 kilograms or $0 \cdot 14$ cubic metres of rock and soil an hour in chalk country. This figure is certainly not highly accurate, but we can be fairly certain it is about right and that ancient Britons or Maoris were not moving only one-tenth of this, 14,000 cubic centimetres (about half a cubic foot) per man-hour, or alternatively ten times as much, $1 \cdot 4$ cubic metres, which would weigh well over two tons! Using the figure of 0·14 cubic metres per man-hour we can calculate that Silbury Hill, a man-made monument 40 metres high near Stonehenge, was built in 275,000 man-days, if each working day was ten hours long. This is the same as 1,000 men working for nine months or 100 men for seven and a half years. It is not necessary to believe that Silbury Hill was a rush job, thrown together in nine months, but what we can say is that it was not impossible for a tribal group to put it up fairly quickly.

Silbury Hill is one of the largest English earthworks. Smaller ones, such as the burial mounds or barrows, could be built in between one and six weeks, depending on the size and the number of people involved in construction. Experiments like that at Overton Down are commonly used by archaeologists to find out more about the possibilities and limitations of past techniques. No one will claim that they have exactly duplicated the past situations, though sometimes we must get pretty close. Experiments show how things *could* have occurred, what unexpected factors need to be taken into account, and what orders of magnitude we are dealing with. Silbury Hill *could* have been built by a quarter of a million people in just over a day, or by an ordinary family in about two hundred years, but given what else we know of settlement sizes and conditions in prehistoric England, it is most likely that a few score or a couple of hundred people were involved. But the experiment itself does not tell us that: we have to estimate that on the basis of other archaeological knowledge.

Experiments and observations of present-day societies all give us a guide to the past, on the assumption that the past has been, generally speaking, like the present. This is the simplest explanation and while it continues to make sense of what we find there seems no reason against using it. So much for the principles; what about the practice?

Most junk from the past is found under the ground. This is because if anything is left above ground it either rots away or is re-used by someone for other purposes—for example, cars abandoned in the streets today are stripped of all their useful parts and the shell is either left to rust, recycled for its metal, or dumped and buried by the local authorities. Only in the last case has it much chance of becoming an archaeological relic.

Once something is buried for a time it is forgotten. People of course forget sooner where they buried garbage than where they buried grandpa or their king, but the principle is generally true. Thus most archaeological research is involved with excavating material from the ground.

Now anyone with a spade and some muscles can dig things up, but to dig up junk so as to get the maximum information from it is much more difficult. This is because people in the past, just like people today, did not bury garbage in neat piles or build their houses (and alter them) with the archaeologists of the future in mind. They dumped their garbage where it was most convenient for them, and built their houses and towns to suit their own way of life. The result, of course, is that any ground that has been occupied for some time is an enormous jumble of material. And the longer people live in one place the worse it gets. Take London, for instance. The centre of London is an area with a radius of about one kilometre round London Bridge, which is itself built close to where a Roman bridge stood nearly two thousand years ago. Central London was walled in by the Romans and such names as Aldgate and Bishopsgate commemorate entrances that have survived, in some cases, for this whole period. Within the area of the Roman wall the present city of London now stands some eight metres above the level of the Roman city. When excavations for new office buildings are made they invariably cut through these eight metres of deposited history. Near Walbrook stream, for instance, a burnt layer near the base of the deposit records Boadicea's burning of London in A.D. 61. A metre or so above it is another burnt layer, relic of the great fire that burned much of Hadrian's London to the ground about A.D. 120. Above that again we find medieval and Tudor pottery and bricks and then the evidence of the Great Fire of 1666. But in addition to these, every tiny area is honeycombed with pits used for rubbish and as latrines, with wells, post-holes for fences, trenches for drains (and more recently gas and telephone lines) and foundations for houses. Each time a pit is dug, soil is disturbed; it and anything it contains are thrown up, mixed with later material, scattered round and sometimes thrown back into the same pit. Later disturbances break through old floors or cut partly into previous pits, and so on—the permutations are endless. In addition there is all the junk that people threw away, or buried, or simply built over the top of. Those of us who live in new houses in new suburbs are probably not used to finding any relics, but anyone who lives in an area settled for even a hundred years will know how much junk is found whenever anyone does any gardening.

The jumble of junk that occurs in every old city, or village, or cave-site where people have been living for hundreds of years can tell a story if it is excavated properly. Archaeological excavation is designed to make sense of jumbles of junk. This is why archaeologists spend so much time digging with trowels and dental picks, why there are so many photographs and drawings and notes—the whole purpose is to be as certain as one can possibly be that the sequence of events has been properly understood, that this wall has been cut through by that trench and not the other way round, that this kind of pottery was found in those buildings and not in the earlier ones. Only when the order in which things happened has been fully understood can the interesting questions be asked with some reason to expect that the answers will be right.

Having found the sequence of events, we can ask how many years ago any particular one occurred. This may be found from written records, which tell about such happenings as the building of the Parthenon of Athens or the leaning Tower of Pisa; or a dated coin may be found in the foundations and we can know that that building is younger than the coin—though not how much younger! But for much of the history of man writing has not existed, while in many cases records were never made or have since been lost. In these situations atomic energy has a peaceful, practical application, especially through radiocarbon-14 dating. Although the actual process of radiocarbon dating is so complex that to have a date calculated costs between $70 and $200, the principles on which it works are quite straightforward.

All living things on the planet Earth are partly made of carbon. This includes our bodies, trees in our gardens, fish in the sea and the crops which feed us. Most of this carbon is a stable, non-radioactive form known as carbon-12, but a small proportion is a radioactive isotope of carbon, carbon-14. We, and every living thing around us, are slightly radioactive. Carbon-14 is constantly being produced in the upper atmosphere by the action of the sun's cosmic rays on nitrogen atoms and it is also constantly decaying at a fixed rate. Every time we eat we take in a small amount of carbon-14 and this replaces what has decayed since our last meal. The same process occurs in all other living creatures. When any living thing dies it ceases to eat or take in carbon-14, but the carbon-14 already in its body continues to decay. Since the proportion of carbon-14 to carbon-12 in living things is stable—or very nearly so—and the rate of decay is known, the age of any dead organism can be determined by measuring the amount of carbon-14 that still remains. If only half the carbon-14 is left, then the object is 5,500 years old; if $\frac{1}{518}$ (0·2 per cent) remains, the object is about 55,000 years old. Beyond that age, radiocarbon dating is not much use, since the problems of measuring such tiny amounts of carbon-14 become too great. With things older than 55,000 years other sorts of radioactive dating methods are used, such as potassium-argon, fission-track, and protactinium-thorium dating. Most of these work on the same basic principle as radiocarbon dating, that is, by measuring the quantity of radioactivity in a sample and comparing it with a modern standard.

Can we check these methods? How do we know they are anywhere near accurate? Radiocarbon dating has been checked against particular historical samples for which we have written dates—such things as medieval houses (about A.D. 1000), Dead Sea Scrolls (about two thousand years old) and Egyptian tombs (three to four thousand years old). It has also been checked against tree-ring counts, ages worked out by counting the number of yearly growth rings found in the trunks of trees, such as some pines, which are several thousand years old. These independent methods of dating show that radiocarbon dates are correct within narrow limits.

When we are dating events that occurred before writing was used, such as a thousand years ago in Australian or North American prehistory, we can only rely on the fact that different dating methods give us about the same results each time. Results are not always straightforward, since all methods are complex to put into practice, and none of them have been as fully tested as radiocarbon, but no glaring inconsistencies have ever been found so far. Anyone who did find one would, of course, be recognized as a clever scientist, so there would be little reason for anyone to conceal such a momentous discovery.

Archaeologists often make guesses about the past. Like a mechanic who thinks the problem with your car is in the gearbox not the crankcase, or the doctor who thinks it's your liver not your stomach giving you trouble, the guesses archaeologists make are based on experience and will sometimes be wrong. But they will also often be right, and further, like the mechanic's and the doctor's, the archaeologist's guesses can be *tested*. We can predict how old a particular monument will be, explain why a town is where it is, suggest what we expect to find before we dig. If we listen, the garbage of the past speaks to us.

# 2. Our Fathers

If a visitor from another planet arrived on Earth today he would have no difficulty in deciding which creatures were men and which were not. He might be put off at first by the minor variations in skin colour, face and eye shape, or height—ranging from 145 centimetres in Pygmies to 200 centimetres in Americans—but the fact that any man and any woman between them can produce a child would soon set him right. He would notice also that all humans speak a language, they all make tools such as spears, bows, guns or atom bombs, and decorate their bodies with clothes and paint. Again, in spite of minor differences, all of us behave more like each other than any of us behave like cows, dogs, monkeys or apes.

These similarities indicate that all human beings form one species, known to biologists as *Homo sapiens sapiens*. As for the visible differences—like skin colour, eye shape, and hair form—between large groups of humans living in various parts of the world—our imaginary visitor would find, if he did some tests, that these were about as significant as the differences between Persian and Siamese cats or between poodles and greyhounds. Further, he would find that the racial differences in humans were much less clearcut than they are in cats or dogs. Three main groups, known as Negro (dark brown), Caucasian (pink), and Mongol (yellow-brown) would stand out, but no other divisions could be consistently made, though groups *within* these major ones could be distinguished in some ways but not in others.

The characteristics that are used today to distinguish between races have probably existed for a long time—whether, like skin colour and hair form, they can be seen by the ordinary person and are individually applicable, or whether, like blood groups and bone measurements, they are scientifically determined and apply to groups. But the problem is that most of them cannot be detected in individual skeletons, or bits of skeletons, which are all that is normally found in archaeological deposits. So although it can be suggested that racial differences of some kind—not necessarily the same kind as we know today—have been around for a long time, what these were cannot be proved for earlier than the last ten thousand years or so, because there are not enough skeletons from the period before this.

But although the minor variations between human groups may be difficult to detect, the main outlines of human evolution are now fairly clear. Most importantly, it is certain that there are no abrupt jumps in the record—each form of early man has its forerunner, none appears suddenly. If we were the direct creation of gods, or astronauts from another world, the history of man could be expected to show sudden changes in form, with a whole new set of genes appearing out of nowhere. Is this the case?

Before answering that question there is one common confusion to be cleared up. This relates to the way we identify and name things. Our everyday classification of the living world is based on what we see: we distinguish dogs from cats, gardenias from gum-trees on the basis of animals and plants that are alive today. Our classifications are useful for dealing with the world around us. But they run into great difficulties when they have to deal with change. There is no doubt that over a couple of hundred generations there will be considerable changes in shape, colour, ear shape or petal size in greyhounds or gardenias, and it is quite likely that if we could see the members of the first and the two hundredth generation together we should be quite happy to say they were different and prob-

ably give them different names. But if we could see not
only the first and two hundredth generations but all those
in between arranged in line it would be quite clear that the
changes had occurred gradually, a little at a time. Then
we should be faced with the problem of where to draw the
line between the two groups. Any answer that we gave
would be arbitrary: one particular feature or another would
be chosen as important and a division made at the place
where it occurred. There is no other way of going about it.

Changes occur in humans just as much as in greyhounds
or gardenias. An actual example comes from a group of
Xavante Indians in Brazil. In A.D. 1970 the 188 Indians
in this group consisted of 37 men, 62 women (all married)
and 89 children. Most men had only one or two wives,
and each wife had only one or two children. But one man,
the chief, had five wives and 23 children, so that over a
quarter of all the children had the same father. So six per
cent of the adults (the chief and his five wives) produced
twenty-six per cent of the new generation. If this process
continues, and the chiefs' children and grandchildren also
produce more than their fair share of descendants, then
within a few generations there will be many more Indians
who look like the old chief and his wives and many fewer
who look like the other members of the original group.
The change won't be suddenly visible in any individual, but
it's easy to see how the group of Xavantes of A.D. 2100
will look rather different, on the whole, to those living in
A.D. 1970. Exactly the same situation occurs when dealing
with the discoveries of early humans. Some of the skeletons
found are clearly not-quite-men, others are nearly-men,
others again are perhaps-men. But the more skeletons that
are found the clearer it becomes that there has been continuous change in man and his ancestors over a very long
period of time. Anthropologists divide these early humans
into groups, but they, like all other biologists, are using a
system that was designed for dealing with the living world
and not with changes over time. So the divisions they make
when discussing changing groups must be arbitrary. This is
not saying that the changes in man's ancestors did not

occur, only that to divide the skeletal material into groups which are thought of as fixed and unchanging is quite unreal.

All over the world today we find only one kind of man —*Homo sapiens sapiens*. As we go back into the past, we can see only a few and insignificant differences back to about 30,000 B.C. All ancient cities, the earliest farming villages throughout the world and the painted caves like Lascaux in France were inhabited by men like us. For most of that period our ancestors were a good deal shorter than we are and lived for only about half our lifespan. A man 180 centimetres or more tall who lives for about seventy years has been a great rarity until the last two centuries or so—and even today is to be found in only a few countries where people's diets have been good for several generations and where doctors are able to cure most illnesses. But in spite of such differences, no cave man or woman would attract even a second glance in a bus or supermarket.

Back beyond about 30,000 years, especially in Europe, a few differences become noticeable, in the person of Neanderthal man. Neanderthal man is the "cave man" of every cartoon and comic strip. He was the first not-quite-human looking fossil to be discovered by scientists, and in 1856, when he was found, they rapidly decided that he was either an ape or a pathological idiot, shambling around unable to stand fully upright, with long arms, a heavy skull with thick bony ridges above his eyes, and covered with hair. This picture persisted for a long time, but now that at least seventy skeletons are known and a number of his camp-sites excavated it is clear that it is ridiculous. Archaeological investigations show that Neanderthal man could hunt giant mammals, including the dangerous cave bear, he stood upright, looked little different from ourselves and lived comfortably in Western Europe during the bitter cold of the last ice age—about the equivalent of living in a cave in northern Norway today.

What's more, the characteristic "cave man" is found only in Western Europe—he was a distinct local race, but no more different from other men of that time than Asians and

Europeans are from each other today. Skeletons from
North Africa and Western Asia dated to about 50,000
years ago look more like us. Indeed, if the men and women
of even 100,000 years ago from Europe, Asia or Africa
were dressed in modern clothes, we might think they looked
a little odd, but most of us would not be aware of any basic
difference. Their brains were the same size as ours, they
stood fully upright and their body proportions were almost
exactly the same. The most obvious differences were in the
face shape and tooth size—the people from that period had
very large teeth and also slightly projecting bony ridges
above the eyes. But they could probably marry our daugh-
ters and sons and have children without our noticing
anything unusual at all.

It is when we have gone back about half a million years
or 14,000 generations that the differences become more
marked and most of us, including the biologists, would
agree we are studying nearly-men rather than man himself.
These nearly-men are known as *Homo erectus* or "upright
man", not because they were particularly honest but because they were thought to be the earliest forms of men to
stand fully upright.

*Homo erectus* fossils have been found all over the old
world—Europe, Asia and Africa. They do not occur in
Australia or the Americas, both of which continents were
settled only within the last 50,000 years or so by modern
man. Over thirty specimens of *Homo erectus* are known,
and they are dated to between 1·5 million and 0·5 million
years ago. The oldest specimens are least like us, the most
recent most like us—about 150 centimetres tall on average,
with a brain size averaging 900 cubic centimetres (modern
average is 1,450 cubic centimetres), teeth rather larger
than ours and with rather heavier, slightly more ape-like
features. These nearly-men lived too long ago for them to
be dated by the radiocarbon method, but some idea of their
age has been given by the potassium-argon technique,
which depends on accurately determining the amount of
radioactive isotope of potassium contained in rocks. All
rocks contain a proportion of potassium, a very tiny per-

centage of which is the radioactive isotope $K^{40}$. Over millions of years this gradually breaks down to the rare gas argon ($A^{40}$). By measuring the amounts of potassium-40 and argon-40 present in a rock sample it is possible to tell how old a particular rock specimen is. Naturally, rocks with high quantities of potassium, such as volcanic lavas, are preferred, since these are easier to measure. Fresh volcanic rocks are also less liable to contamination by argon from the air. So when an old camp-site, or human bones, are sealed below some volcanic materials, we can say they must be older than that material. If they are above the lava, then they must be younger than it. Fortunately both Central Africa and Indonesia, where many of the *Homo erectus* specimens have been found, are highly volcanic areas and so a number of specimens have been dated.

*Homo erectus* was also a successful hunter and meat was a regular and significant part of his diet. This has led anthropologist Loring Brace to suggest that he was hairless —possibly the first of man's ancestors to be so. Brace points out that all other carnivores, such as lions and cheetahs, rest during the hot part of the day and hunt in the early morning or evening; man, on the other hand, tends to hunt in the middle of the day when he can rely on the animals he is hunting, such as deer, becoming exhausted by the heat. Man can do this because he has a hairless skin and many sweat glands, allowing him to stay cool; other animals get hot in their fur coats. But of course as man gradually lost his body hair he would be more likely to get badly sunburnt and develop skin cancer unless some other change occurred. So Brace suggests that this is also the period when nearly-men first develop dark skins, for these contain more of the pigment melanin, which acts as a natural filter against sunburn. Hairless, black men are the most efficient hunters—and they can also hunt at a time when other hunters, like lions, are less likely to be hunting them—safety first, too!

All the men and nearly-men so far discussed are usually called *Homo*—they are enough like us to be recognized as relatives. But once we get back about two million years ago or so—perhaps 1·5, perhaps 2·5 million—the beings who look rather like men, standing upright but able only to run rather than stride, are so different that they can no longer be called *Homo*. These near-men, or ape-men as they have been called, are known technically as Australopithecines. Most specimens come from Central and Southern Africa, but they probably existed in all tropical areas of the Old World. The bones from Africa reveal that these near-men were quite short, averaging only about 120 centimetres in height and weighing between 20 and 35 kilograms. Brains were small, too, proportional to the bodies: they have a volume of about 450 cubic centimetres, compared with modern brains at 1,450 and ape brains at about 300. As well as standing upright these men were efficient tree-climbers—a good escape from ferocious animals—and normally lived for only about twenty years. The other important feature about Australopithecines is that they do not have projecting canine teeth. If you look closely (not *too* close!) at the mouth of any ape you will see that on either side of the front of the jaw there is one very large tooth. These teeth, the canines, are used in fighting and are essential for survival. Man has these teeth, but they are only the same size as all the rest, for he has replaced them with guns, bows and arrows and similar weapons. Weapons may be used for hunting also, but this is not essential. Man, after all, can catch young or weak and small animals by hand, just as chimpanzees do. But weapons of some kind are essential for fighting. The fact that Australopithecines do not have large canine teeth must mean that they have replaced them with some kind of weapons—not guns, but probably wooden spears and throwing stones. Australopithecus is obviously on the way to becoming man.

It is only in the last few years that earlier and even less man-like fossils which still have some semi-human traits have been discovered. These come from periods as far back as fourteen million years and may also be the ancestors of some of the apes. Or the apes may have developed on their own for even longer; there is still a great deal of argument and not very much evidence on which to base statements.

But one thing is clear. For the last five million years at least there have been no sudden changes in human evolution. Australopithecines grade into *Homo erectus*, who in turn, by easy and barely perceptible changes, becomes *Homo sapiens*. Each of the fossil skeletons that has been discovered supports this picture, none stands out as being unusual or wildly different. Theologians may wish to argue that at some point in the development man became "truly" man by being given a soul. But souls do not fossilize and they cannot be dug up, so archaeologists say nothing about them.

# 3. The Man-made Past

There are approximately four thousand million people on the earth today. We are the most obvious of the inhabitants of this planet, both because of our numbers and also because of our culture—our tools and weapons, cities and towns, beliefs and memories. We are the only animal to possess this complex way of staying alive, and all humans have a basically similar culture.

What caused this? Are we all, with our thousands of languages, our enormous cities and our complicated governments, just the creation of beings from some other world? Part, perhaps, of a gigantic cosmic experiment of some extra-galactic scientist?

If this is indeed the case, then there will be something strange about our past. It will show inconsistencies—jumps in the record. We should find, for instance, that cities appeared suddenly and are not preceded by large towns or they in turn by villages; we should find that agriculture does not develop as a product of trial and error over thousands of years, but appears overnight like some new and different cuckoo in mankind's nest, the earth. Did man develop in this sudden, directed way, or is each of our advances the product of human sweat and human intelligence?

Only 150 years ago, until about 1800, nearly everyone in our Western civilization believed that man's development *was* sudden, that the first agriculture and cities did appear almost overnight, and that even man himself had been created by God only six thousand years ago.

The rose-red city of Petra, built three thousand years ago, really was "half as old as time" as the poet said. But for the last hundred years and more, archaeologists have been looking at the junk that the history of man has left behind.

The information that has been dug up, especially since 1900, in Africa, Europe and Asia demonstrates beyond doubt that man and his ancestors have been on the earth for millions of years. It shows also that each one of man's advances did not result from a sudden and easy acquisition of new knowledge, but from trial and error by many people over hundreds or thousands of years. Sometimes they succeeded, and the results of these successes are part of our history; at other times they failed, which is why archaeologists can find "lost" civilizations and forgotten cities. Before writing, even the successes could be forgotten quite quickly, which is why we do not know the names, for example, of the first discoverers of America or Australia. But with archaeological work we can discover something about when and how man's successes and failures occurred.

The oldest man-made products that survive are stone tools, simply fist-size pieces with a few chips knocked off them. The sharp edges were used for cutting meat, skinning animals, and chopping wood and bone. We know these stones are tools both because they are made in a regular pattern, unlike any pattern normally found in the naturally broken rocks we can pick up in streams or on beaches, and also because they are found at camp-sites where perhaps-men lived. As well as stone tools, these camp-sites contain animal bones that have been broken open to get at the marrow, and sometimes other, larger stones used as a base for a windbreak.

Camp-sites where the first tools have been found are mostly in Central Africa and some date to as much as 2·5 million years ago. One such site is FLK I at Olduvai Gorge in Tanzania, which was occupied about 1·6 million years ago. It was an area about seven by five metres, the size of a modern living-room, beside a small lake and probably under a shady tree. Within this area over a thousand tools, the stone chips from making them, and broken bones were found. Around the camp was a zone eight feet (2·4 metres) wide with almost no finds, probably where a brush windbreak existed, while outside this again the finds were much more scattered and consisted of nearly all the larger, chunky pieces of stone, as well as big bones like shoulder-blades. The explanation is that large stones and bones were uncomfortable to walk or sit on and were tossed out of the camping area. Seventy per cent of the animals eaten at FLK I were deer; other animals include pigs, horses, tortoises, rats, birds, snakes and fish.

The perhaps-men who lived at FLK I and other similar sites made stone, bone and probably wooden tools, and this is all that remains in the ground today. But finding a camp-site with a windbreak, along with other evidence that it was used for more than overnight sleeping, is a good indication that a near-human pattern of life was being established. No living apes, man's closest biological relatives, establish home bases where the old or sick animals or females with young may stay during the day and have food brought to them; perhaps-men did this 2·5 million years ago at least.

But in other ways their life was still very similar to that of the apes. For instance, it was not until nearly two million years later that fire was used. The perhaps-men who lived at Olduvai, Sterkfontein and other African sites had no hearths to warm themselves by or to cook food in. They were like tropical animals who lived in the open and ate their food raw. Their successors, living less than a million years ago, who made stone tools only a little better, were able to live in cooler climates. They used fire for warmth and to cook meat, but particularly to gain access to caves. Before man had fire, bears, hyenas and other killers could dispute his occupancy of caves; with fire, he was master. It can be no accident that the oldest fires are found in caves such as Escale and Vallonet in France and Verteszöllös in Hungary some 750,000 years ago; there is no evidence for the use of fire before this. Caves were used, of course, to shelter from the weather, and men always lived near the entrances, where it was light during the day. The use of

fire had one other important side effect—it increased the
length of the day by removing man's dependence on the sun
for light. This meant that night-time could be used for talk
and planning, ceremonies and story-telling. At first man
did not create the fire he used but obtained it from natural
sources—accidental fires started by lightning or the spon-
taneous combustion of coal or shale-oil—and then carried
it with him by firestick from place to place.

Some of the bones found in cooking hearths and rubbish
dumps of half a million years ago are those of near-men.
Many of these bones have been broken open to get at the
marrow and are also burned from cooking. Some skulls
have the foramen magnum—the hole at the base where the
spine joins on—broken open to get at the brain, an
especially tasty part. But although near-men were often
cannibals, they may none the less have had a good deal of
respect for the dead persons they ate. We know today that
people in many societies believe that to eat part of someone
else is to absorb something of his or her power, strength
and wisdom: a similar belief is present in Christianity in
sacramental form.

The earliest actual burials of dead people, which are the
first real demonstrations of respect for the dead that we
can see, occurred only about 70,000 years ago, and then
offerings were frequently put in graves also. The body
might be sprinkled with red ochre powder to give it the
colour of life; joints of meat, stone tools and shell necklaces
were sometimes included to make the dead person feel at
home in his new life; at Shanidar in Iran the dead man
was even laid to rest on a carpet of flowers, 50,000 years
ago or more. Whatever may have been the case before this
time, burial of the dead implies a very human concern for
one's relations. We cannot tell whether Neanderthal man
believed in an after-life, though this is implied by the use of
colouring material and the supply of provisions for the
dead. Similar burials have been found in France where
all the bodies were buried in a flexed position, with
the knees drawn up to the chin. There may have been
religious reasons for this, but also, of course, it is the

attitude in which a body takes up the least space, so that less dirt has to be dug out of the ground to make an adequate grave.

The colouring materials found in burials are not the oldest evidence of man's use of paints. In a French beach-side hut 300,000 years old some near-man (or woman) left a pointed piece of red ochre, rather like a piece of red chalk, which was probably used for painting bodies or one of their wooden tools. But the use of colour to paint pictures on cave walls only occurs much later than this. The oldest cave paintings so far known are found in Europe and are about 35,000 years old. They appear at the same time as the first jewellery, consisting of necklaces of pierced animal teeth and fish backbones, ivory bracelets and rows of coloured stone beads sewn onto clothing.

The paintings in the caves of Western Europe are dominated by life-like pictures of animals, mostly large animals like elephants and bison that men might hunt. There are almost no representations of plants, very few of men, and nothing that might be called a landscape: all this implies that we are looking at the art of a hunting society and that this art was an important part of the hunt. The fact that most of the paintings are up to a mile inside completely dark caves, where men never lived, also implies that this art was probably of some religious significance. From our point of view of course, the fact that the paintings were hidden away in dark caves, where the atmosphere was very stable and only very small changes occurred in the local environment, has meant that they are preserved for us to see. The only other art of equivalent age, that found in Koonalda cave in Southern Australia, is similarly hidden nearly half a mile inside the cave, away from light, weather and other disturbances.

Rock paintings from other parts of the world—northern and southern Africa, America, India, New Guinea and Australia—are all made in the entrances to caves, under rock overhangs or on boulders. They are exposed, even if only slightly, to rain, wind, dust, light, and temperature and humidity variation. Like the paints we use today, those used by rock artists fade, crack and flake off; after several hundred years there is little left of any painting. So it is because of its location that the cave art of Western Europe seems to be the oldest in the world; other much older art may well have been destroyed.

It is quite clear that during the last 100,000 years or so there has been a speed-up in the rate at which man's culture has changed. Whereas the first, simplest stone tools were used for at least 1·5 million years without any changes, later forms have lasted for a much shorter time. Also, more tools were invented—fine stone points, bows and arrows, for example—while the first art, jewellery and musical instruments are also found during this period. Why should this be?

If it were the result of extra-terrestrial influences, we should expect to find many new things appearing at once, probably at only one or at a very few places in the world, and spreading out from there. In fact, we find the opposite. The first musical instruments are bone whistles from North Africa, 65,000 years old, while the earliest art in different places varies widely in age and content. About 30,000 years ago in Western Europe a number of new small stone tools were invented. These appear to result from more economical ways of using raw material—from the same block of stone a worker could get perhaps five times as many sharp edges for use as knives, scrapers and spear-points as he could before. Ten to forty feet (three to twelve metres) of cutting edge could now be obtained from a single pound of stone. This invention was taken up rapidly in Europe—why not, if it was more economical? But the same economical methods existed well before this in Western Asia, while in Africa the same result was slowly achieved, using rather different methods, between 20,000 and 10,000 years ago. So changes and new ideas are not the monopoly of any group or any particular time.

The increasing rate of cultural change can be linked most plausibly to two facts, increasing knowledge and slowly increasing population. Knowledge feeds on itself— the more complex a culture the more options are open, the greater the number of possible discoveries; more people means more minds to think of these possibilities, to interact with each other and spark off changes. Thus when there were few near-men and they had only a few crude wooden and stone tools there were few possibilities for changes, and these occurred only rarely, but each discovery and change meant that man had a larger cultural store to draw on and combine in various ways. This is why, over the centuries and millennia, new tools and new ideas appear with increasing frequency. We are familiar today with the fact that there has been more change between 1950 and 1973 than there was between 1900 and 1950: the increasing rate of change is also visible in prehistoric times.

Increasing knowledge and increasing population helped men to settle in more parts of the world. The perhaps-men (Australopithecines) and the near-men (*Homo erectus*) evolved in the tropics of Africa and Asia and, within the last million years, spread to colder parts of the same great continental mass, to Europe and northern Asia. But they did not reach the Americas, Australasia or many of the world's smaller islands, such as Madagascar. Sea crossings of twenty miles (32 kilometres) or more were beyond them, while the bitter cold of the Bering Straits area also kept them out of America. It was only within the last 50,000 years that these areas were settled, apparently in all cases by *Homo sapiens sapiens*, modern man. Radiocarbon dates show that Australia and New Guinea were occupied 30,000 years ago, or a bit more, while the first men in the Americas probably arrived only about 20,000 years before Columbus and Eric the Red. The smaller islands that were farther away from continents and required longer sea voyages to reach them were settled even later; most Pacific islands, for example, were reached within the last four thousand years.

The settlement of the new continents, in particular, required man to adapt himself to a whole new world. In Australia, for instance, the animals—kangaroos, wombats and other marsupials—were very different from those he knew in south-east Asia and hunting methods had to be

changed to cope with them. Once there, too, each group of
men had to develop their societies without outside help:
there is evidence only of very rare contact between the
major continents after first settlement. If there were much
contact we should expect to find many more similarities
between societies in different parts of the world. For
example, more efficient transport using the wheel should be
found in the Americas, and the agriculture there should
use some of the main plants that were domesticated in
south-west Asia. We should probably expect to find agriculture introduced into northern Australia where the soils and
climate, at least, do not differ very much from areas in
Indonesia and New Guinea where agriculture is common.
If each area did not learn to develop essentially on its own,
but acquired such techniques as farming and building from
a single source, there should be many similarities between
these things in all parts of the world. How similar *is* the
world-wide history of man?

The first farmers and herders are found only about ten
thousand years ago and they appear at roughly the same
time in at least three separate areas—the Fertile Crescent
(Mesopotamia), Mexico, and south-east Asia. But the
change to this way of life was not accomplished suddenly
—it took at least four thousand years in each place.

South-west Asia about 12000 B.C. was the home of
hunters and gatherers, *Homo sapiens* who looked like us.
The women collected a wide range of seeds, nuts and
vegetables, as well as snails and other small creatures,
while the men hunted wild sheep, goats, deer and cattle.
It is possible that some of the animals were being herded,
too, like reindeer in Lapland today. In some areas the
environment was especially good and wild grasses were
abundant, allowing quite large settlements to be formed.
Such sites as Mallaha in Israel or Zawi Chemi Shanidar in
Iran about 9000-8000 B.C. were fair-sized villages with
stone-built houses. People relied heavily on harvesting—
thousands of small flint blades with the glossy edge that
comes from cutting many grass stalks have been found—
but the actual seeds they were eating still came from wild

grasses. This can be clearly demonstrated from the size and genetic make-up of the grass seeds found in these sites.

When man begins to control the breeding of plants or animals he removes them from their natural state and this affects their genetic characteristics. Man selects larger seeds because these give him more food; the animals he begins to herd tend to have more meat and wool because he selects for these characteristics. In all cases he probably keeps alive—and breeding—plants and animals that would not survive in nature, thus increasing genetic variability in the group. Such changes were only beginning to be visible in plants such as wheat and barley and in sheep, goats and dogs by 8000 B.C. It is not until about 7000-6500 B.C. that there is evidence of plants and animals that are clearly under man's control. Those plants and animals have formed the staple crops of Western civilization from then until today; we have domesticated no new animals for food for eight thousand years.

The same pattern of gradual development is even better documented for agriculture in Mexico. A series of sites excavated in the Tehuacan valley produced several thousand maize fragments dating between 5000 B.C. and A.D. 1500. These show how maize, the basic crop of American agriculture, became like it is today. Maize, often known as Indian corn, is a native of Mexico and in its wild form, as remains show, has grown there for tens of thousands of years. Wild maize-cobs are only about 19-25 millimetres long and, like the seeds of many wild grasses and plants, are very uniform in size and shape. Each has about fifty-five edible kernels. They have been found in sites dated as recent as 5000 B.C., along with other evidence which demonstrates that people were gathering wild foods and hunting wild animals. Two thousand years later the cobs have been selected for increased size, but are still only about 40-50 millimetres long and contain about 135 kernels each. The size increase, however, is the only change: in all other characteristics it is still wild maize. It was only when this maize was crossed with a near-relative known as *teosinte* that the botanical characteristics of the plant changed. As well, larger maize continued to develop. By about two thousand years ago there were several different races of domestic maize, all of them bearing corn-cobs about as large as those of the present day; by a thousand years ago the number of races had increased to ten.

The story of maize is one of very slow beginnings, of slowly increasing size, and then, after several thousand years, the development of an increasing range of races and types. These changes are consistent with a slowly developing understanding of the potential and breeding characteristics of plants; they are *not* consistent with a sudden invention which sees a rapid change and a fixed end result.

We have less complete evidence from south-east Asia, but one fact is important: the crops grown there were completely different again from those of other parts of the world. Such roots as yam and taro, as well as sugar-cane and bananas, were the staples, in contrast to the grains of Mesopotamia and the maize and beans of Mexico.

The development of agriculture in each of the three regions relied exclusively on plants and animals that had wild forms in that area. Wherever we have evidence, any changes occurred slowly. Villages did not suddenly appear fully reliant on agriculture, but rather large camps grew larger and a bit more permanent, a few plants were protected from local animals and allowed to flourish. For thousands of years men relied partly on hunting and gathering as well as agriculture and domestic animals.

Once agriculture was fully established, however, and men both relied upon it and understood it fully, plants and animals could be taken out of the localities where everything began, and where they were at home, and could colonize new areas. The agriculture that started in south-west Asia, for instance, was confined to areas of Mediterranean climate —Turkey, Greece, Egypt and Crete—until about 5000 B.C., since men knew only how to look after plants and animals in a limited range of ways. But about 5000 B.C. there is a sudden and very rapid spread right across Europe of men possessing agriculture and domestic animals, so that the hunters and gatherers of England were forced into becoming farmers and herdsmen by about 3500 B.C. What happened was that some groups of farmers gradually came to understand how to farm in a European rather than a Mediterranean climate and this then opened up a whole new country for them—a new frontier like the opening of the western plains in America in the nineteenth century.

The same kind of process occurred in other parts of the world, and throughout Central America, India, northern Africa and Asia farmers spread and hunters were incorporated, more or less forcibly, into the new system. Today there are only a few thousand hunters and gatherers left in the world—our industrialized agricultural society will no longer permit them to exist, even in deserts or jungles. But this spread of agriculture over the whole world has taken ten thousand years from its first beginnings.

Metal-working, another important invention, develops later than agriculture, and it also occurs in different forms in different parts of the world. In south-eastern Europe, for instance, copper sources are found in many mountainous areas, and the earliest metal-working, about 4000 B.C., involves no more than hammering into shape naturally occurring lumps of ore. Small objects such as beads and fish-hooks were made in many places.

Metal can be produced from copper ore only if it is heated to 800°C. This temperature was being attained in the kilns of several groups of clay potters in the Balkans about 3700 B.C. The copper they heated became a fused mass, which was then shaped by hammering. For melting and casting copper a temperature of 1050°C is required and this temperature was produced only in the kilns of potters who were making graphite-painted pots in one small area of the south-east Balkans (the Gumelnita culture) about 3500 B.C. The technique of high temperature firing was first developed for pottery and then applied to metals. The discovery that these high temperatures allowed copper to be smelted was made in an area where ores and fuel were plentiful, where earlier forms of metal-work were well known and where agriculture was sufficiently well developed to allow permanent settlements to be formed.

A number of factors had to be present simultaneously before the invention could occur. That this was a local invention is conclusively proved by the objects being made: they bear no resemblance to those from other metal-working areas to the south and west.

Metal-working in the Americas seems to have begun in a similar way about 300 B.C. Cold-hammering of copper is widely found among both North and South American Indians, but smithing is much more restricted in occurrence. The first bronze-working, requiring a tin-copper mixture, seems to have developed in Bolivia, in close proximity to the tin sources. Here, however, the relationship to high-quality pottery-making is less clear.

What about city life? Villages and even small towns occur early in the period of agricultural development. By 7000 B.C. the town of Jericho covered ten acres (four hectares) and the inhabitants built a dry-stone wall six feet (two metres) thick and a stone tower over thirty feet (ten metres) high for defence. Similarly in Peru by 2500 B.C. many villages of five hundred to a thousand people existed and could be the basis for later, larger settlements, while in China well-built large villages existed by at least 2500 B.C. and probably a good deal earlier.

We may see cities as the logical outcome of village and town growth based on agriculture. As agriculture developed it could feed more and more people while using the same area of land. As the number of people each farmer could feed increased and as population numbers continued to rise there was increasing conflict with closer neighbours over water-rights, trespassing animals and land claims. The efficient way to deal with these disputes was through a centralized legal system, once communities became too large for face-to-face contact. Larger populations also put greater strains on resources, and made long-distance trade more costly and difficult. In some societies vitally necessary commodities—salt, stone for axes, knives or grain grinders —had to be brought in from outside. While it would be fairly easy to organize person-to-person trade on a small scale, as many New Guinean societies do even today, to move a larger quantity of trade goods would require greater organization and protection. It is notable that in Mesopotamia (the Tigris-Euphrates valley) and among the Maya of Central America, both societies in which trade was vital, the earliest cities were built in just those areas which were farthest from essential resources. It is almost certain that the cities contained the merchants', soldiers' and priests' quarters and were centres from which powerful men could organize long-distance trade and its protection.

Cities also tended to develop first in major river valleys, where flood controls and irrigation works were needed to make farming continuously successful. Such control over water supply (or over-supply) was not necessary in areas where rainfall provided a sufficient but not excessive supply for agriculture. But in such valleys as those of the Nile, the Indus and the Yellow River, water comes irregularly through the year; at times it must be kept in the river by additional levee banks, at times it must be channelled and directed through dry fields. Such needs require a developed administration, with power to enforce its orders and defend its rights, and so the city as an administrative and organizational centre grows, gains powers and eventually dominates the countryside. As people and power come together, they outgrow a tribal organization in which people and problems are few enough for everyone to have time to participate in most decisions. Decisions come to be made by some people and the work carried out by others; jobs become specialized, for there are enough people around needing particular kinds of goods to allow full-time professional workers to make a living: cobblers stick to their lasts rather than being also part-time farmers, fighters and law enforcers, as they were in smaller communities. Once society is too complex to allow everyone to be involved in everything, the rise of the administrator is almost a certainty, but while the pattern of the origin and growth of cities is similar throughout the world the form and character of man's various civilizations are so different that each was clearly a local development. Each one developed in its own distinctive style and tradition. It must be stressed, however, that although the outlines and style of each main civilization are known there is little information on the details in some cases, such as India and China.

In the flood-plains of the Tigris-Euphrates valley, the area known as Mesopotamia, at the head of the Persian Gulf, the earliest settlements date from about 5000 B.C. These were villages with square temples set on small artificial hills made of mud bricks. The village people made pottery, farmed irrigated fields, and marked their ownership of objects with picture stamps and seals. As population grew villages combined to maintain access to irrigation water and to defend their trade routes, so that by 3000 B.C. there were about twenty city-states, small areas of land each with a defensive-walled city where perhaps fifty thousand people lived—merchants, priests, soldiers and craftsmen. Many of these people were not divorced from the land, but while living in the city spent part of their time cultivating fields just outside the city walls.

Priests and temples dominated the Mesopotamian cities. Each main temple owned much of the farm land and employed farmers, potters and many other specialists, taking their products and redistributing them to others—very much like an enormous household or commune. But the temples were not egalitarian; each was staffed by professional priests who administered the business and took their cut of the produce. It was they who invented the first writing to enable better management of the temple business. The world's first written documents are not prayers or stories, but accounts.

The god of each city was also an important part of its defence against intruders, but naturally enough he (gods were nearly always male!) required help, so war leaders, who eventually became kings, were important in each city. The kings lived and died in some splendour—the royal tombs of Ur, for instance, contained carts and chariots, harps and bowls, as well as many court servants all dressed in their finest gear who were killed when the king died and were buried with him.

Wars in those days, of course, made money for the

victors as well as ensuring their water supplies and protecting their trade routes. Defeated cities had to supply tribute in goods and slaves, and their citizens had to pay taxes to the new overlord and his god, so kings often fought not only in defence of their territory but also to increase their power. After some time there were only a few cities that had had a number of continuously successful kings, and these few eventually formed larger states, controlling several cities. By about 2300 B.C. Mesopotamia was united under one ruler whose empire controlled as much wealth and as many people as possible and whose desire was to keep within the country all sources of raw materials that were essential for the empire's survival. That aim remained dominant for the next four thousand years, until the Ottoman Empire of the nineteenth century.

The Egyptian civilization developed very differently. It was centred on one river, the Nile, which flooded reliably every year and brought new soil to the fields, but needed little in the way of massive canals or dykes for irrigation or flood control. Moreover, the Nile was bounded on either side by the desert, so societies and their power-seeking rulers could look only in one direction—along the river. There is no evidence of walled towns or massive temple buildings in the early stages of the Egyptian civilization, as there is in Mesopotamia; rather, all along the Nile we find large villages which are then, in the space of only a couple of hundred years, united under one king. We do not at present know how and why this occurred. Egyptian legend has it that the final unification was of the two kingdoms of Upper and Lower Egypt, and for many generations the Pharaoh was always spoken of as king of both countries (compare the Queen of the United Kingdom—the former kingdoms of England and Scotland, with Northern Ireland and Wales); but the evidence for the existence of the two kingdoms in Egyptian history is very scanty. There is also no evidence that outside invaders first brought the country under one rule. While there was considerable trade between Mesopotamia and Egypt as early as 3000 B.C., and Egyptian hieroglyphics (picture-writing) may be based on

Mesopotamian ideas, the rulers from earliest times were clearly Egyptians—they looked and dressed like Egyptians and only rarely do foreign goods occur in their palaces.

From the beginning Egypt was united under one king who was himself also seen as a god. It was the royal court that was the main source of wealth and power, not the cities and temples, and the specialists and craftsmen were to be found at court. Similarly, the Pharaoh's government controlled all trade and the economy of the country, and it was this high degree of central control over resources and people which allowed each Pharaoh, like Tutankhamun, to fill his tomb with gold and other precious objects.

While Egypt was a civilization without major cities, and Mesopotamian cities grew up jumbled round temples like many south-west Asian cities today, the first cities in the Indus valley of western India (Pakistan) were laid out in a distinctive and orderly grid pattern. Cities like Harappa and Mohenjo-daro, which were built about 2300 B.C., consisted of a central fortified citadel, standing on a man-made platform of mud bricks twenty metres high, overlooking a chessboard layout of broad streets and oblong blocks of houses. The citadel included a temple, the city's grain store and a very large bath, thirteen by seven metres, lined with bitumen. Each house was a series of rooms built round a courtyard to which there was only one entrance, with a doorman's room, and each had its own brick drain connecting it to the main city sewer. A similar degree of official municipal control is present in all the small towns of the area, too; each has its grid layout and its town drains.

The Indus civilization developed very rapidly and its remains from towns to pots are very similar over a large area of western India. How did this happen? Until we can read the Harappan writings, still in one of the world's unread languages, we cannot really know, but we may guess that this kind of similarity does not arise by chance. It would be a fair bet that the Harappan civilization grew up from the defensive and trading needs of large and growing farming populations. As in Mesopotamia, the initial push towards city life, with all that it implies, probably came from

competition, not co-operation. But the Harappan civilization differs from the Mesopotamian in that unification
probably occurred quickly and urban planning was rapidly
imposed.

Competition also formed the original unifying factor in
China, where, despite the distinctively Chinese nature of
all material remains, we can see that the first really large-
scale societies were fighting city-states. Along the Yellow
River, as along the Tigris and Euphrates, there was a clear
and ever-urgent need for flood controls, and it is just here
that the first Chinese cities are found. These cities are
notable for such discoveries as oracle bones—shoulder-
blades and similar bones heated until the surface became
crazed, with the cracks then being interpreted as answers
to questions about fame and fortune—bronze axes, carved
jade figures and elaborate burials of kings with their servants
and chariots. These finds, as well as the everyday pots,
knives and houses, demonstrate that the Chinese urban
societies were created by Chinese people as a natural expression of their current needs. There was occasional trade
with India and even with the West, as shown by such finds
as coins. Marco Polo was the last, not the first, of a long
line of travellers to Xanadu! But since the Chinese always
considered foreigners to be barbarians their influence within
China was limited.

In the New World, the Americas, the strongest evidence
for the independent origin of civilizations is the fact that
their agricultural base—maize, beans, squash, chilli, sweet
potato—was totally different from that found anywhere in
Europe or Asia, while the form and organization of cities
is also distinctive. In two areas—Mesoamerica (southern
Mexico, Guatemala, Honduras) and Andean South
America, centring on Peru—cities and empires grew up
from about 1000 B.C. In Mesoamerica the earliest pattern
is one of temple-centre cities staffed by priests and rulers
who drew their food and wealth from surrounding scattered
farms. Villages were rare and the cities themselves were
mostly just temples and a few residences. Later, in the
highland areas, such places as Teotihuacan are real cities,

with large numbers of people living off intensively culti-
vated gardens near by. But over the whole of Mesoamerica
the basic political unit was one of small states ruled by
petty kings. These states were in constant military competition and when occasionally one became dominant it would
prosper through taxes imposed on the others. The Aztecs
were the last people to dominate the area in this way. The
states organized the trade that distributed such vital resources as stone—commonly used for knives, axes and
other tools by most people—and salt. Elaborate markets
were supplied by human pack-trains, for these societies had
no domestic animals that could carry goods. Each state was
dominated by gods, particularly agricultural gods, whose
favour had to be kept if men were to live well. Their
temples towered over each city in both lowland and highland areas and their priests developed complicated and
accurate calendars to predict the seasons and the behaviour
of the gods as well as to regulate elaborate rituals.

The temples were sometimes pyramid-like, but with ex-
ternal stairways leading to temples at the top. Unlike
Egyptian pyramids, all of which are solid stone and contain
tombs within them, the Mesoamerican ones are of earth,
rubble or mud brick faced with stone and are mostly solid.
The strange tomb inside a rectangular terraced Mayan
pyramid at Palenque is an uncommon form, but it is not
unique.

In the Peruvian area the first small-scale cities are found
along the coast among people who were primarily fishermen
but who also did some farming. They used stone for buildings before 2000 B.C. At Culebras an entire hillside was
levelled off into broad terraces faced with stone blocks, and
stone-built houses, partly underground, were erected on
each terrace. The building stones were of locally available
basalt, which occurs in regular blocks that require no shaping before being fitted together into walls. Elsewhere in the
region people used different building materials—blocks of
fossil coral, whale backbones or, more commonly, mud
bricks and irregular boulders—but building with stone was
easy and frequent in this stony area. Here, too, we find

pyramid-shaped constructions dating from about 2000 B.C., but these also differ from those found elsewhere. For example, at Rio Seco excavations have shown that one pyramid began as a house with mud-brick walls; later the walls were filled up with boulders and earth and another house built on top of it. After this had been done several times the pyramidal mound was covered with sand and blocks of stone were stood upright on top of it. Pyramid it may have been, but in this case it occurred by natural growth rather than original design.

As with other civilizations, a reliable and storable food crop was essential for survival, growth and development in the Andean area. This crop was maize, which, along with beans, not only provided an adequate diet for the farmers but could easily produce a surplus to feed priests, rulers and construction workers. Here, as in Mesoamerica, the earliest major centres were not cities where many people lived, but temple centres, which were used and supported by surrounding farmers and villagers. At La Florida, in the modern city of Lima, for instance, there is a pyramid built out of natural stone blocks and surrounded by smaller temples and buildings, but it was for occasional use and not for living in—this can be said because no rubbish dumps or house remains occur in the area. The pattern of temple centres with only a small permanent occupation of attendant priests is found in both highland and coastal areas of Peru; much work went into the construction of these centres, but, like many of our own churches, they were used by most people only a few times each year.

About 900 B.C. a new religion spread through much of Peru. We know of it through material remains called the Chavin style and it can be recognized by very similar carvings and temple buildings over a wide area. The temples were elaborate buildings on high platforms, always built to a similar basic design but of varied materials. In the highlands shaped stone was used both for buildings and their decoration, while on the coast temples were made of field stones or mud bricks and decorated with plaster and clay. The Chavin remains are the earliest in which any pan-

Peruvian similarity in such minor goods as pots and carvings has been observed, and it is from this time also that we
have the first evidence of long-distance trade in the area.
The Chavin cult, however, was not associated with a military
or political conquest; it seems to have been primarily a
religion which simply drew together and developed what
was already present—stone-built temples, elaborate carvings
of human-animal figures—rather than a totally new style,
government or way of life.

The history of Peru after about 500 B.C., shows several
periods of partial unification under religious or political
domination with intermediate periods when local powers
were important. But throughout the period there is a basic
similarity and continuing development within the civilization. In the highlands, the large well-watered valleys were
rich enough to support many people, and about 200 B.C.
cities developed in several places—Pucara, Huari, Tiahuanaco. These were surrounded by villages and small towns,
and were not just ceremonial but residential centres. In the
coastal valleys small cities were formed. In all areas there
was sufficient prosperity and food surplus to allow for
massive temple building, either in stone or mud brick, and
temples, often in the shape of a pyramid, are common over
the whole region. About A.D. 470 the whole of Peru and
considerable areas beyond it were finally unified under the
Inca empire. The Incas could draw on two thousand years
of experience and they controlled enormous resources, so
that their great stone-working feats such as Cuzco and
Sacsahuaman are the culmination of a tradition rather than
an unexpected development.

Was there contact between the great civilizations of the
Old and New Worlds? Were the American cities and
civilizations the result of copying the achievements of China
or India or Egypt, or were they created by rulers from
those places? So far, there is no evidence that there was any
major political or cultural influence on the American
civilizations from anywhere in the Old World. While there
are some remarkable similarities in particular features—
we can say, for instance, that the art of making paper and

cloth out of tree-bark in the Americas was almost certainly introduced from Indonesia about 1500 B.C.—all links between civilizations seem to have resulted in the exchange of single items of manufacturing technique or design. If cities and civilizations were introduced to the Americas from outside we should expect to find at least some of them like cities in the old world. We should expect to find the wheel and animal power used in transport, something that never occurred in the Americas. Further, American cities do not appear suddenly; they develop out of temple centres in particular areas where rich lands could support large non-farming populations. Temple centres occur very widely and their inhabitants do not continuously require large quantities of food, so they are suited to the scattered homestead pattern of American farming life. Cities are preceded by towns and villages, all of which grew out of a long-term agricultural development. It should also be noted that the methods and styles of building are locally derived and depend on the quality of available materials; they do not appear to copy extra-American forms.

The question of trans-Pacific contacts would not be so difficult to answer definitely if writing had been more common, but for many years writing was used to record accounts only, not history or literature. In Mesopotamia and Egypt it developed from that into more complex records, but in the Americas it was used primarily for calendars and astronomical predictions; we could not expect it to record a few visitors from other societies. Certainly the Incas and earlier societies had historians who memorized great events, but in the absence of written records these memories were usually lost when that particular political organization collapsed. Only the Inca histories that were recorded by the Spanish conquerors still survive today.

Civilizations appear to result from complex causes. Among the important factors we may list environment, food production, fairly dense populations, occupational specialization, the development of classes of rulers and administrators, trade and warfare, resulting in the spread of knowledge as well as the concentration of power. The expansion of many societies was limited by such things as lack of water, barriers to communication like mountain ranges, and low population numbers in some areas. It is because all these factors play their part that each civilization is different, not only in such obvious things as the way they picture gods, paint pots or organize calendars, but also in how their societies function—temple centres with villages or tightly packed cities, priest-kings or god-kings, loose or tight political control. If civilization is unnatural, imposed on us by some outside force, why is it that each society, each group of men, produce a different result, and a result whose sources can be traced back into their own history for thousands of years?

The near-men and near-women who hunted and gathered their food for millions of years, the men who developed agriculture, metal-working and city life, were all part of a continuing process of change, as we are today. We can trace our Western civilization back through the Romans and Greeks to Egypt and Mesopotamia; the Chinese have a separately recorded history of more than two thousand years and an archaeological record many times longer; in the Americas Westerners conquered Inca and Aztec, each of whom can be shown to be the final stage in a long sequence of economic change and political growth. When we look back at our past there are no sudden and inexplicable jumps in the record, no changes which do not grow out of man's own efforts and actions.

# 4. Pyramids and Pyramidiotics

There are about eighty pyramids in Egypt and twice as many in Sudan to the south, but of the 240 the best known are the three large pyramids at Giza, just outside Cairo. The largest of these, the Great Pyramid of Cheops, was one of the seven wonders of the ancient world.

This pyramid is outstanding in size and in the accuracy of its construction. It is also said to embody many significant measurements, unusual proportions, even predictions of the future. Is this in fact the case? Is the pyramid of Cheops very different from the other pyramids in its size, construction techniques or precision? Does it alone convey unexpected measurements and unusual propositions? Or is it only the best made among many?

To answer such questions is not always easy, because written Egyptian records, whether in the form of old letters and court documents or of wall-paintings, only infrequently record the methods used in building pyramids. That activity, like some others in ancient Egypt, is not described. What we do have as evidence is the remains of the pyramids themselves, including some unfinished ones, which often tell us most about building methods. There are also many discoveries of the tools used, the quarries where stone was obtained and the villages where workmen lived, while there are some wall-paintings showing the cutting and dressing of stone and the transport of enormous blocks by water and over land. We can also see how the stones were measured and aligned and experiment with the methods that appear to have been used to see whether they actually work. How was a pyramid built?

The first act was to select a site. This was not done at random. *All* the pyramids stand on the west bank of the Nile, closest to the setting sun. They also stand above the level of the flood-plain, where they can easily be seen, both by men and by the gods—including the sun-god. In addition, none is built more than a mile or so from the Nile, flood-plain and many of them are far closer to it than this, within easy reach of the water—and ships—during the annual flood. If strange forces were used to transport the stones, why were all the pyramids built in locations where there was relatively easy access to them by water?

The site had to be on solid unflawed rock, for pyramids weigh millions of tons. The site had also to be level, so that the building would stand securely. Since most natural rock is not exactly flat, it had to be levelled artificially, and this was done with great accuracy. The base of the Great Pyramid of Cheops, for example, slopes less than one centimetre in 230 metres, an error of about $0 \cdot 004$ per cent. How was it done?

The chosen area was first cut into by a grid of ditches which were filled with water. The floors of these ditches were then chiselled away until each was precisely the same depth below the surface of the water. The water was drained away and the rest of the area was taken down to that level. In some cases only the outer parts of the pyramid's base were levelled and a small rocky hill was left at the centre to form the core of the pyramid. This is the case with the Great Pyramid, as well as some others. Using a hill like this would save time and effort in construction.

Once the site was levelled, the building would be laid out. Egyptian pyramids are all built as a square, and the ideal form was that the sides of the square should face north, south, east, and west. All pyramids are built like this, with one exception in which the corners face in these directions. The directions are not, of course, compass points —the Egyptians did not have magnetic compasses—but based on true north, the direction in which the Pole Star rises, and the point about which other stars rise and set in the northern hemisphere.

The orienting of pyramids was done with great care. In the Great Pyramid the four sides are in error by only 2 to 5½ minutes of arc (a minute is one-sixtieth of one degree); other pyramids are less accurate—they might be up to half a degree out. Most of these errors would not be detectable by us with an ordinary compass, we should need surveying equipment. How was this amazing accuracy achieved?

On the east side of the Great Pyramid are some trenches about 170 feet (51·85 metres) long but, with stone linings, only some 35 inches (89 centimetres) wide. As Sir Flinders Petrie says:

> No better device for observing accurate transits [the moment at which a star crosses the meridian] could be made than by stretching a thin rope from end to end and looking past the rope to the reflection of the rope occulting [hiding] the star in its reflection from water below.

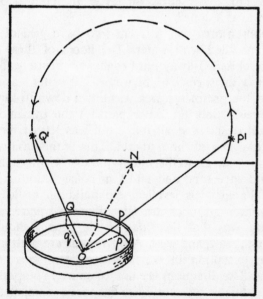

*A method of discovering true north*

If a ring opening were included in the rope and a lamp below lighted the reflected rope the conditions would give the fullest accuracy of naked eye observations.

Another possible method, but one that would leave no traces, is the creation of an artificial horizon—a wall, levelled by using water, over which the rising and setting of several stars could be observed. Half-way between their rising and setting points is north. Once north is discovered, the other three directions can be worked out by the use of right angles.

Similar care, but with the same slight inaccuracies, occurs in the laying out of the sides of the pyramids. In the Great Pyramid the sides are not all of equal length—they vary by seven to nine inches (18-23 centimetres) between the longest and shortest sides. This is an error of under one in a thousand. The error probably occurred because the measuring ropes, made of palm fibre or flax fibre, stretched when in use. When measuring over long distances it is very difficult to keep exactly the same tension on a cord. Try it some time, and see how nearly you can duplicate a measurement of 50 metres.

Egyptians, of course, did not work in feet or metres, but in cubits (or ells), hands and fingers. Four fingers equalled one hand, and seven hands one cubit (ell). A cubit is equal to about 20·62 inches (52·36 centimetres). Pyramids were sometimes built with base and height in exact cubit multiples, but more often they were not so precise. The Great Pyramid, for instance, is 440 cubits a side and was probably 280 cubits high. The second pyramid near by (Chephren's) is 410 cubits a side and 272 high. The third pyramid, in the same area, that of Mycerinus, is 200 cubits a side and 124 cubits 2 hands high. But the three smaller pyramids built for Cheops's queens have bases of 92 cubits 6 hands, 92 cubits 2 hands 1 finger, and 88 cubits 1 hand 2 fingers respectively. Other large pyramids are often built in exact multiples of cubits also.

We know about Egyptian measures from many sources. One of them is the marks found on the pyramid and temple building stones themselves. The marks may be cut into the stone or be simply red paint lines made by a builder's string being flipped against the stone, in the same way as is done by bricklayers today. The marks look like this:

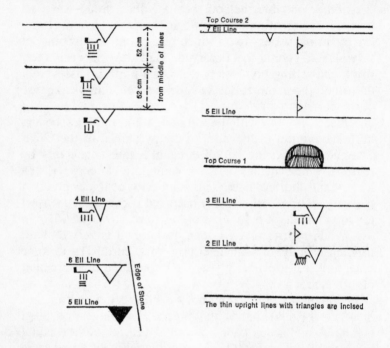

These marks come from the temple built at the foot of Mycerinus's pyramid at Giza, but marks of the same kind have been found in many pyramids and quarries. If pyramids were built in some mysterious way one wonders why their builders needed such simple everyday instructions and guidelines. Only ordinary men need these aids.

Most of the stone used in each pyramid came from nearby quarries. The cores of the Giza pyramids, for example, are made of a coarse limestone containing many fossil shellfish of a particular kind (nummulites). This limestone is found in the area where the pyramids are built so that is where the quarries must be. Careful searching has shown that the giant hole within which the Sphinx is set is in fact man-made. The Sphinx is carved on a small outcrop that was left in the quarry. The volume of the quarry we can still see would be sufficient to provide most of the stone used in the pyramids. It was, of course, sensible to quarry most of the stone from the nearest area, to avoid having to move it any farther than necessary. Only people concerned with time and effort, who knew that pyramid building was not child's play, would worry about such simple matters.

Once the core was built many pyramids were faced with a fine white limestone which came from the Tura quarries on the east side of the Nile, the opposite side from the one the pyramids were built on, but not very far away. The quarries are still visible today, with long tunnels that follow particular seams of the best stone. The quarrymen were sensible enough to leave pillars of stone standing so that the roof would not collapse. The stone was sawn or split into blocks in the quarry. The Egyptians had copper saws and chisels at the time the pyramids were built, and marks of their use have been found on many blocks. They also used wedges and hammers; sometimes wooden wedges were swelled with water and metal wedges may have been used also. Wedge slots may still be seen both in these quarries and in the granite quarry at Aswan.

The quarrying method at Tura consisted of first cutting a shelf-like slot at roof level for the full width of the seam. Then a workman got into this slot and worked downward at the back of the block while others cut away at the sides. Finally the block was split away at the base along the natural cleavage planes, removed down a ramp, and the whole process started again. The blocks were taken from the quarry to the building site in their unfinished state. Each block was marked with the name of the gang that cut it out, and many of these names survive, painted in red on the inner face of the blocks. Names have been found on blocks in most pyramids and temples. Those from the pyramid temple of Mycerinus include "The working gang, Mycerinus-is-drunk", and "Mycerinus-excites-love", while on blocks in the Great Pyramid are such names as "The working-gang, Cheops-excites-love", and "The-white-crown-of-

Khnumkhufu-is-powerful". These names are written in hieroglyphs:

Most of the limestone blocks from the Tura quarries weighed between two and five tons, but some of the blocks obtained from quarries close to the pyramids weighed up to two hundred tons. How were these blocks moved? They weigh as much as a hundred motor-cars all crammed into a volume as big as an ordinary household sitting-room. No records or paintings of remains of railways, blocks-and-tackles, pulleys, cranes or other machines have ever been found in ancient Egypt. How was all this stone transported?

The method is recorded in a wall-painting in the tomb of Thuthotep, an official who lived a thousand years or so after the Great Pyramid was built. This painting shows a giant statue, weighing at least sixty tons, being pulled overland on a sledge. Four ropes are tied to the front of the sledge and 172 men pull on the ropes. The statue is bound to the sledge and there are pads between the rope and the statue to stop rubbing of the carving. A man stands on the statue's knee to chant a pulling song—like a sailor's shanty for pulling up anchor—and keeps time by clapping his hands. At the front of the sledge another man pours water or oil under it to make the ground slick so that the weight will slide easily. He is kept supplied by three carriers, seen

below. Three other men carry a roller or block, possibly to
stop the statue slipping back or forward when the pullers
rest.

In the same tomb there is an inscription recording this
great work. It reads in part:

> A statue 13 cubits high, of stone from Hatnub. The road
> it traversed was an extremely difficult one. The dragging
> of the great statue along it was excessively hard work
> because the ground was very hard and stony. But I made
> the young men, the miners and the quarrymen, come and
> build a road for the statue. Behold, this statue was more
> valuable than anything else and with this my tomb is
> complete.

Sledges pulled by men were used to move large stones not
only in ancient Egypt but in other ancient societies. Almost
exactly similar scenes are found in Assyria, where giant
winged bulls and other carvings had to be installed in
temples and palaces.

But other methods apart from manpower could also be
used. In the debris left by the builders of the pyramid of
Sesostris II at Lahun there are many short, thick rollers
with rounded ends, made of trees that grow in the Nile
valley. These rollers are crushed along their sides in the
pattern that occurs on wood used for moving heavy weights.
At the Tura quarry there is also a carving of a stone block
on a sledge being pulled by a team of oxen, looked after by
three men. But it is unlikely that oxen were in common use,
since their upkeep was expensive.

For stone blocks on sledges to be moved easily there must
be fairly flat roads and ramps for them to slide on. Surfaces
would need to be smooth and firm, and the inclines up or
down not too steep. Remains of such roads and ramps have

been found at the granite quarries at Aswan, as well as in the debris of at least four pyramids, including that of Chephren's pyramid at Giza. The most complete of these ramps is that found sloping against part of the "buried pyramid" at Saqqara. This unfinished monument was only discovered in the early 1950s and comprises the lowest two steps of a step pyramid, the earliest form in which pyramids were built. Against the western side, nearest the quarry from which the stones for it came, there was a ramp of rock and earth.

From this and other remains it seems probable that most pyramids were built with one major supply ramp covering the whole of one side. The gradient of this ramp would be between one in twelve—according to measurements for a ramp given in a written scroll of fairly late date—and one in eight, which is the actual slope of a ramp used during the building of the pyramid temple of Mycerinus. As the building grew the ramp would be both raised and extended so that the same slope was maintained.

Around the other three faces of the pyramid were much steeper embankments, the tops of which were wide enough to permit the movement of men and building materials, but which were much too steep for anything to be pulled up.

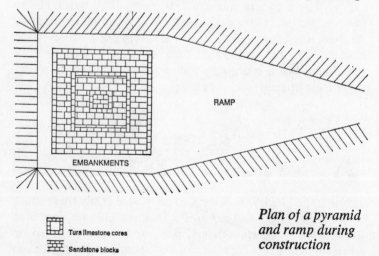

RAMP

EMBANKMENTS

Tura limestone cores

Sandstone blocks

*Plan of a pyramid and ramp during construction*

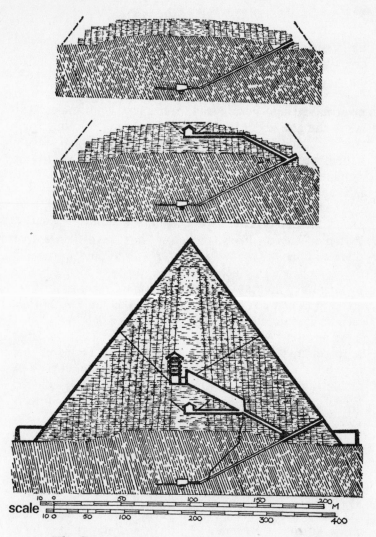

scale

*The Great Pyramid of Cheops in cross-section*

Remains of these embankments have also been found at Saqqara.

Pyramid building started from the centre. Blocks of stone smoothed on the bottom surface were laid in the form of a square, which was gradually extended outwards. At regular intervals the square was perfected by adding a Tura

E

limestone course cut to correspond with that in the platform below. That is, each pyramid was composed of a series of nested pyramids, one inside the other.

As well as being pulled with ropes, stones were also manoeuvred into position by levers, used both under their edges and also under knobs (or bosses) left projecting from the blocks for this very purpose. Such knobs would usually be removed once the stone was in position, but a number of examples, some showing signs of use, have been found in incomplete buildings.

The blocks used to cover the outside of the pyramids were cut to fit very exactly, especially in the case of the Great Pyramid. It seems likely, though we have no evidence, that this was done at ground level by master masons who could check their work by actually trying the fit of blocks before moving them into position on the pyramid. Only in this way could joins between blocks accurate to one-hundredth of an inch be guaranteed.

Stones were cut with copper saws and with chisels. They were squared and surfaced not only with T-squares and plumb bobs but also with facing plates and paired rods. A facing plate is a sheet of flat material covered with red marking fluid which is held against the flattened surface. Any small projecting irregularities will be touched by the red marker and can be removed. The other instrument used was a set of T-shaped rods each of exactly equal length. Two would be held upright some distance apart and the third moved between them. Line of sighting alone would be sufficient to give a very accurate result.

Once the pyramid had been completed the ramps and embankments were removed slowly and the outside limestone given a proper final dressing. This would be done mostly by small emery blocks and other abrasives, which have been found in the builders' debris. During the building the inner chambers and passages were constructed according to carefully designed plans, but once they were completed their final treatment would probably have been left until later, since the main entrances at least would have been covered by the ramps and embankments. Perhaps some work inside was possible, entrance being made through devious passages left primarily for workmen to escape after the funeral and the sealing in of a king's corpse.

How many men did it take to build the pyramids and how long did it take them? We have no exact figures about this at all. There are a number of traveller's tales, including those of the ancient Greeks and Romans, but since they were writing two thousand years or more after the pyramids were built we cannot expect their evidence to be too reliable. What direct evidence do we have?

At the northern pyramid of Sneferu at Dahshur two blocks have been found with dates on them. The blocks are both casing blocks of Tura limestone used for the outer surfacing of the pyramid. The dates refer to particular years during the king's reign. One block is at ground level in the north-east corner and, because of the way pyramids were constructed, must refer to the year in which work began. The date is the twenty-first year of Sneferu's reign. The other block is half-way up the face of the pyramid and bears the date of the following year. The only possible inference is that this pyramid was built in about three years. Its volume is about three-quarters of that of the Great Pyramid, so that was no small feat. No other inscriptions with such precise information have been found, but such rapid building does seem to be unusual. There is some evidence to suggest that Pharaohs went on building their pyramids for many years and some who died unexpectedly never completed all the works—Mycerinus's temples, for instance, were completed by his son and successor, who skimped the job pretty badly.

We have little direct information about the way the work was organized. Gangs of about 250 workmen were probably the basic unit, with an army-like chain of command to transmit orders. Many men were probably only employed for short periods when their farms did not need them—the use of "forced" labour of this kind is almost universal before the invention of money and is the ancient equivalent of tax payments. Most people probably regarded it in much the same way as we regard taxes and national service—as a necessary evil.

But it also seems likely that the master-masons and other skilled workers would have been employed full-time on the project, and behind the pyramid of Chephren, at Giza, Sir Flinders Petrie has found the buildings in which such workmen lived. They are long galleries built of rough pieces of limestone bedded in mud, with a mud or mud-and-lime plaster. At the end closest to the pyramid the gallery walls are joined to a cross-wall which runs almost parallel to the pyramid wall itself. Each gallery is about 93 feet (28·3 metres) long and just over 9½ feet (3 metres) wide. The walls stand to a height of about 7 feet (2 metres). The total length of gallery space is about one and a half miles (2·3 kilometres) and it has been estimated that they would provide barrack-like accommodation for about four thousand men.

For short periods many thousands more men than this would certainly have been needed, but they probably camped in temporary huts for their two or three months' work. The gangs into which they were divided were the basis for a work organization quite different from the kind we are used to. We should expect the quarry gang, boat gang, pulling gang, and building gang to be separate groups, with stones being passed from one to the other as work progressed. But this is not, apparently, how the Egyptians did it. Apart from the master-craftsmen, who remained on the one job throughout, it seems likely that each block of stone was quarried, moved, shaped and fitted into place by the same gang of workmen, whose name was written on the stone. This would give each man a sense of participation in the final product, which our methods do not, and ensure that each knew that his contribution mattered to the Pharaoh's well-being.

We have no detailed accounts of the workmen's lives from the time of the pyamids. The barracks which Petrie excavated provided little information about their everyday life. But from a thousand years or so later, at the time of king Tutankhamun, we have a clear picture of the workmen involved in building his enormously rich tomb. They lived near the Valley of the Kings in a large walled village which had, as well as houses, a public square with a well and a police station at the gate. Each house had an owner, whose name was carved above the door. The most important find, however, is many fragments of pottery which the Egyptians used as we would use scrap paper—to scribble notes to each other and to record things they wished to remember. Pottery fragments (*ostraca*) were used because paper had not yet been invented and papyrus, a type of paper-cloth made from reeds and used for writing on, was expensive and difficult to make.

The *ostraca* record the route the gangs of workmen walked to the Valley of the Kings to begin their ten-day working week in camp. These workmen were not slaves. We read, for instance, that individuals had days off to take a sick donkey to the vet or to bury an aunt. There are applications for promotion and for new tools to replace those worn out. One foreman's accounts show the number of wicks issued to his team for the oil lamps used to light their work underground. Oil lamps of the same kind have been found in the rubble of many pyramids, while actual examples were found in the pyramid of Sesostris II at Lahun. They were used for lighting the work in the tomb chambers. If properly trimmed, or shielded, oil lamps do not smoke much more than candles.

As well as work accounts, many aspects of daily life are revealed on the *ostraca*. Correspondence between neighbours, schoolchildren's homework corrected by a teacher, illustrations of popular fables like the wolf and the kid, even the method of drawing lots for particular duties and elections, are recorded. The ingredients and amount of the day's rations are also specified. On one occasion the men complained that they were weak and starving because their rations had not arrived, and they immediately went on strike. Hardly the behaviour of slaves!

It seems very probable that the workmen who were employed full-time on pyramid construction a thousand years or so earlier lived in much the same sort of way—

Egyptian life, after all, did not change very greatly. But in
the pyramid period the permanent employees were assisted
by seasonal labourers, probably for the period when the
Nile was in flood. That was the time when least work was
required in the fields and when the river came closest to
the pyramid so that the transport of stone was easiest.

Pyramids were built essentially as tombs, to preserve a
king's body after death. The preservation of bodies after
death was an essential part of Egyptian religion, which saw
life after death simply as a continuation of earthly existence,
but one in which all goods, services, and even food had to
be supplied from this world. Although the new life was that
of a spirit it was necessary for the spirit to have a base, a
home in which objects, or drawings of them, could be part
of its life. This belief in an after-life continues throughout
the Egyptian civilization and such tombs as Tutankhamun's,
a series of underground chambers rather than a pyramid,
express the same set of beliefs. All royal and private tombs,
even those of the poorest people, contain some provision for
the world the dead were entering. The kings had the biggest
and best tombs, but these were only an extreme expression
of the normal practice in ancient Egyptian society. Queens,
for instance, sometimes had smaller pyramids, while many
hundreds of nobles and officials built themselves rock-cut
tombs and small temples, often with elaborate decoration
and furniture to make their life after death as pleasant as
possible. The average peasant was buried with a little food
and clothing to ensure some comfort in the life to come,
though no average man could afford a lavish tomb.

Most pyramids have some fragments of the material—
furniture, jewellery, food—that was buried with the
Pharaoh, but in none have the whole contents been preserved. This was because most tombs were robbed within
a few hundred years of the Pharaoh's death. The passages
that the robbers made to bypass the granite blocks used to
seal the passages have been found in many pyramids. Some
of the tomb robbers were caught and taken to court; their
interrogation has been preserved and it is clear that they
made a regular business of it. This is why most pyramids

have little remaining in them; the gold and other valuables were taken out and recycled into the community. But the fact that the Pharaoh's names appear on many hundreds of the building blocks as well as the presence of their symbols and paintings of their activities show conclusively that they were built for their use alone.

Why were the royal tombs built in the form of pyramids? There is no simple answer to this question. It is, of course, the easiest way to build a very large and strong building; the shape is such that it will last "for ever", and this was certainly the concern of the Pharaohs, who wished to continue living their life-after-death. But this seems too mundane to be the full explanation. What else is involved?

One of the many different ways by which the spirit of a dead king could approach heaven was by a staircase. One of the spells used in religious ceremonies states that "a staircase to heaven is laid for the king so he may mount up to heaven thereby", and the earliest pyramids are just like a staircase—the so-called step pyramids with four to six giant steps ascending to an apex in the sky. Most later pyramids also embodied the step idea—the nesting series, if cut off at different levels, would be a series of steps—but they altered the outer surface to the smooth ramp-like structure that is so well known. This was almost certainly to symbolize the rays of the sun shining down on the earth, as they may be sometimes seen on a cloudy afternoon. In this natural phenomenon the rays are in fact frequently at the same apparent angle as the sides of most pyramids (about 51 degrees) and it seems very likely that the pyramid was intended to be a permanent representation of the sun's rays which the dead Pharaoh would use to ascend to the sun-god. Several spells refer to this idea. Number 523, for instance, reads: "Heaven has strengthened for you the rays of the sun so that you may lift yourself to heaven as the eye of Rē." By changing from the simple step pyramid to the smooth ramp-like one the tomb became more closely associated with the sun-god and the dead king's divinity was more firmly asserted: he was not just a mortal who was specially privileged with his own heavenly staircase, but was a living associate of the sun-god and could use some of the god's methods as well as those of normal mortals.

But, it has often been said, although the ancient Egyptians built the pyramids in accordance with their religious beliefs, none the less the Great Pyramid also contains many strange measurements and formulae and was built by methods and according to designs that the Egyptians themselves did not understand. Is this true? What signs and predictions does this monstrous building contain?

The Great Pyramid of Cheops, the largest of all known pyramids—though not by very much—and its measurements have been used as a basis for saying that the Egyptians knew the value of $\pi$, the distance from the earth to the sun, the weight of the earth, and the future course of world events, including the destruction of life on this planet. Some of the calculations involved in these theories are of great complexity and I do not always understand them. So it seems best to start with the simpler ones, especially since many of the more complex ones are based on the same data.

1. It has been claimed that the height of the pyramid multiplied by $\pi$ ($3 \cdot 14159265$ . . .) gives a result equal to the length of any two of the four sides measured at ground level. A similar claim has been made for the area, divided by $\pi$. Now $\pi$ is the relation between the radius of a circle and its circumference ($2\pi \times$ radius = circumference) and the exact value was worked out only within the last few centuries. Did the Egyptians really know this figure, too? First, the measurements used:

The height of the Great Pyramid is 280 cubits or 5,774 inches (approximately). The length of each side is 440 cubits or 9,073 inches (approximately).

For a start, it is quite obvious that the area (that is, length $\times$ length = 193,600 square cubits) divided by $\pi$ will not give an answer anywhere near the height—the figure is actually 61,624. But it is certainly true that if we multiply the height by $\pi$ we get an answer very close to twice the base length. Thus $280 \times 3 \cdot 14159 = 879 \cdot 645$ cubits. Not quite 880 cubits, but fairly close. Does this mean the Egyptians knew the exact value of $\pi$? Not necessarily. We all know that as an approximation for $\pi$ we may use the fraction $22/7$. Now $22/7$ actually equals $3\cdot142857$, and 280 cubits $\times$ $3\cdot142857 = 879\cdot99996$ cubits—closer to 880 cubits than the answer we get when we use the more exact measurement of $\pi$. So that it seems very likely that the Egyptians knew the approximation $22/7$, which could be worked out by geometry, but not the more exact, mathematically calculated, value of $\pi$. The use of the approximation $22/7$ is quite common in pyramid building. One of the three small queens' pyramids built beside the Great Pyramid uses it (base 88 cubits 1 hand 2 fingers, height 56 cubits 5 hands) as does the "blunt pyramid" of Sneferu, while the measurements of at least six others, including the two other large ones, those of Chephren and Mycerinus, at Giza, approximate to it quite closely.

It is not clear *why* this ratio was used so widely. It may have been something to do with the way Egyptians measured, but it may also have had something to do with volume calculation: if the pyramid is treated as a cone then it is much easier to work out how much stone would be needed and so to plan the whole business of building. However, in Rhind Mathematical Papyrus, dated about six hundred years later than the main period of pyramid building, there are elaborate instructions for calculating the volume of a pyramid. It is possible that these mathematics were employed by the pyramid builders, but we do not know that this is the case.

2. There is also the claim that the height of the pyramid multiplied by a thousand million corresponds to the distance between the earth and the sun. There are problems, of course, with both measurements. Of eighteen different attempts to measure the earth-sun distance made between 1896 and 1962, none came within each other's error limits. There is some uncertainty about the exact height of the Great Pyramid, which had its top thirty feet or so stolen in antiquity, but here we can project the sides fairly accurately

to a point. If we work with a realization of these limits to our calculations we may consider the following facts:

The distance of the earth from the sun is, on average, 93,000,000 miles. It varies during the year from 91,450,000 to 94,560,000, for the earth does not go round the sun in a circle, but in an ellipse. The height of the pyramid, according to Petrie's accurate survey, is 5,773 inches. If we multiply that by a thousand million we get about 91,114,200 miles—less than the shortest distance from the earth to the sun at any time of the year! Or take the calculation the other way round: if we divide the average distance of the earth from the sun by a thousand million the answer comes to 5,892 inches, a difference of 119 inches or about two per cent—not really very accurate. And we might ask why the pyramid builders would have needed to express such a distance anyway? Further, apart from the measurement itself—which we, not the Egyptians, made—there is *no* evidence that the Egyptians realized that the sun was a far-away ball of fire. To them, as we can see from many wall-paintings and texts, the sun-god Rē was a deity who journeyed across the sky in a boat, and boats for the Pharaoh to accompany Rē were frequently buried close to the pyramids or cut into the rock near them. The boat of Rē journeyed across the sky, thought of as the top of a world which was shaped rather like a giant shoe-box, on the floor of which men carried on their everyday life.

If one wants to, one can juggle figures in all sorts of ways. For example, the height of the Eiffel Tower in Paris is 29,992 centimetres. This is almost exactly one-millionth of the speed of light (29,977,600,000 centimetres a second). The difference is about 1 in 2,000 or five-hundredths per cent. Can this be chance, or were the builders of the Eiffel Tower in possession of this mysterious information? Why would they express this relationship in the tower, built in 1889 for the Paris Exhibition, if it were not to exhibit the marvellously accurate knowledge they possessed?

3. The weight of the Great Pyramid has been calculated at about 5,923,400 English tons, and this is supposed to equal the weight of the earth divided by a thousand billion

$(10^{15})$. One of the problems here is how we calculate the weight of the pyramid. No one has ever counted all the blocks in the building, let alone measured them so that their weights can be calculated. Petrie estimated that there were 2,300,000 blocks, but others have said 2,600,000. No one knows precisely how much space is occupied by the natural rock core at the central base of the pyramid. Some people take account of the spaces occupied by chambers and passages, others do not. Most people are generally agreed that the blocks weighed *about* two and a half tons each, but some are clearly much larger, while the granite used in the construction of the underground burial chambers would be much heavier. So that any estimation we come up with is bound to have a pretty large margin of error. If we take the two measurements given, then the weight of the pyramid is probably somewhere between five and three-quarters and six and a half million tons, but it may be as little as five and a quarter or as much as seven million. This is a large range.

The weight of the earth is said to about $6 \times 10^{21}$ English tons—that is, six thousand trillion tons, and the two weights do stand in the stated relation roughly and approximately. So what? There is a lot of leeway in both calculations and we have no idea of the significance of the discovery anyway. Why would Egyptians or astronauts want to build a monument of stone blocks to express rather roughly a figure that they—if no one else—would already know and that we, the first people to rediscover it, calculate by quite different means?

The "discovery" of these measurements, like the prediction derived from the same building that the world will end in 1853 (or 1890, 1927, 1954, 1981) is based most of the time on inaccurate measurements and making the answer fit. Sometimes it doesn't—Petrie found one man filing down a particular stone boss in a pyramid because it was the wrong size for his theory!

But even if the pyramids do not predict the future and are based on no more than simple geometry, they are nevertheless amazing, enormous pieces of engineering. Even more amazing, in some ways, were the red granite obelisks, weighing several hundred tons, on which the Egyptian Pharaohs recorded many of their exploits in war.

Obelisks, tall needle-like pillars of stone, were carved at Aswan. They are actually the symbol of the sun-god, Rē, and were erected by kings both in his honour and in their own. Some of these obelisks are enormous: they are solid pieces of hard stone weighing several hundred tons and standing just under a hundred feet high. How were these giant monuments cut, transported and erected? Was this within the powers of men?

The obelisks that are still standing in Egypt and those taken from there to the Vatican, London, Paris, New York, and other places give us no hint of the methods used. They stand, shiny, hard and enigmatic, with little hint of their history.

But in the quarry at Aswan there is still a partly finished obelisk, left by its builders several thousand years ago. They left it because the stone was faulty: an unexpected fissure in the granite meant that the completed monolith would be too weak ever to be moved and stood upright. Even when they attempted to save some of the work they had done by reducing the intended size, they found still other fissures which made it impossible. So there it lies today: 137 feet (41·75 metres) long and with an estimated weight of over 1,100 tons. The builders' loss is our gain, for they abandoned an uncompleted work, still showing many of the methods that they used. Other methods can be determined from the surrounding quarry where there are many traces of working.

When an obelisk was planned the first problem was to locate a large enough piece of solid stone. To do this small test shafts were sunk into the rock so that its characteristics at depth could be inspected. Two such shafts still remain at Aswan. Then, too, the surface rock, which was heavily weathered, had to be removed. This was normally done with fire and water—a fire was lit on the stone to heat it up and then water was thrown on it, causing it to split. At Aswan there are many pieces of burned granite as well as other

Levelled area on the north side of the Great Pyramid

Granite casing blocks on the pyramid of Mycerinus

Rock paintings from the Tassili, Sahara Desert

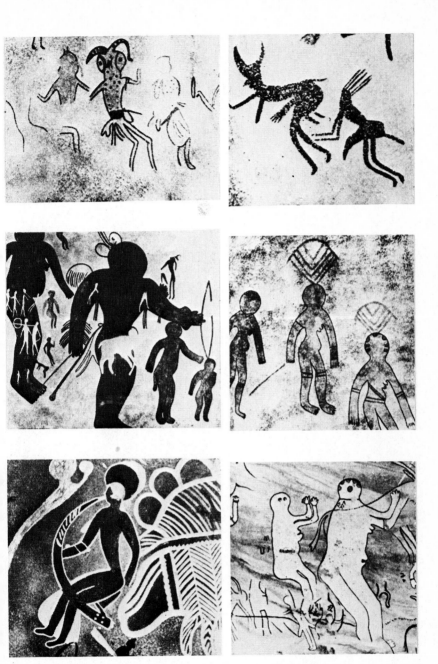

Rock paintings from the Tassili, Sahara Desert

Wandjina figures from north-western Australia

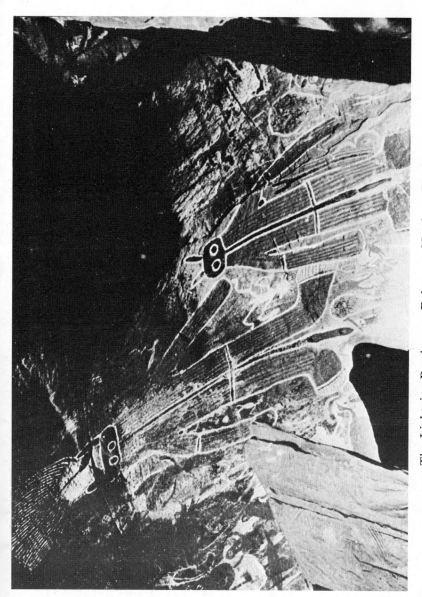

The Lightning Brothers at Delemere, Northern Territory

Carvings at Val Camonica, northern Italy

Strange mural by Neil Burley on one of Sydney's largest buildings, Kingsgate at Kings Cross

The Nazca lines in relation to the Palpa River valley

Nazca lines overlapping one another

The giant trident of Pisco

traces of fire. At times wedges might also be used to split away the rock pieces. There are many thousands of wedge slots of all sizes to be found in the Aswan quarry. Some of them were used for wooden wedges, which were swollen with water in order to split the rock. Others are smooth, tapered slots which were probably used with metal wedges, since wooden ones would just pop out of them when wet. A series of metal wedges hammered in in turn would be just as efficient as wood, and we know that the Egyptians did have wedges of this kind.

One thing that is not very clear is how the wedge slots themselves were cut. Copper tools were common through-out the period of pyramid building, but ordinary copper does not cut hard granite well. If cast metal tools are hammered, however, this hardens the metal considerably, though not permanently. Hammering a copper tool can raise its hardness from 87 to 135 (Brinell scale), and in this state it would be much more suitable for working stone. Some of the copper tools found in Egypt appear to show evidence of hardening in this way, but because the change is not permanent this is not always easy to determine.

Copper was too rare and valuable—and not really strong enough—to provide all the mining tools, and the Aswan obelisk was shaped and outlined mostly by the use of stone hammers. These were round or oval balls of dolerite weigh-ing around 12 pounds (5·5 kilograms), which have been found in their hundreds in the Aswan quarries.

Stone hammers were used both for flattening the surface and for excavating the rock around the obelisk. We can be certain of this from the form of the surface and the trench, not smoothly cut but showing a series of scoop-like depres-sions. Each stone hammer was probably mounted in a wooden handle and used by a gang of three or four men, one of whom stood in the trench to guide it and clear the dust away. Hammering is certainly not a very speedy method, but it works. The method has been used in the Aswan quarries within the last century, and R. Engelbach also experimented with the hammers. He calculated, on the basis of an hour's work, that it would take a year or more to cut out the Aswan obelisk, working a twelve-hour day. This may be compared with the historic Egyptian records which say that the obelisk erected by Queen Hatshepsut at Karnak took seven months to construct. The Karnak obelisk is less than half the size of the unfinished one and would have taken much less time.

We have direct evidence about the removal of obelisks from their quarrying place. Sometimes they were simply moved out sideways by pulling them on skids or rollers, but the unfinished obelisk, like some others, was made in a trench, and other methods of removal would have had to be used. The most likely theory is that levers consisting of tree-trunks some twenty feet long were inserted on either side and the block rocked back and forth while men inserted packing underneath it so that the whole block was gradually raised. About thirty levers a side, with fifty men pulling on rope attached to each, would be sufficient to move the block.

Obelisks would be moved on sledges down the roadway which still exists at Aswan. There are Egyptian pictures of an obelisk being pulled on a sledge—just like the statue—and also of not one but two obelisks being taken down the Nile on a boat. There are also written accounts of the same thing. Thus Ineni, who was the superintendent of buildings in the reign of Tuthmosis I (about 1500 B.C.) has the following inscription written in his tomb: "I inspected the erection of two obelisks and built the 'august' boat of 120 cubits in length and 40 cubits in breadth for transporting them. They came in peace, safety and prosperity and landed at Karnak."

Having been brought to the site, the obelisk had to be set upright. This cannot have been easy, since the monolith would snap very quickly if not supported under its whole length during erection. We also know that once upright an obelisk could not be moved, since there is an example at Karnak of a monument standing askew on its base—something no architect would have allowed if he could have corrected it. The most likely method of erecting obelisks is that they were slid off the end of an embankment into a

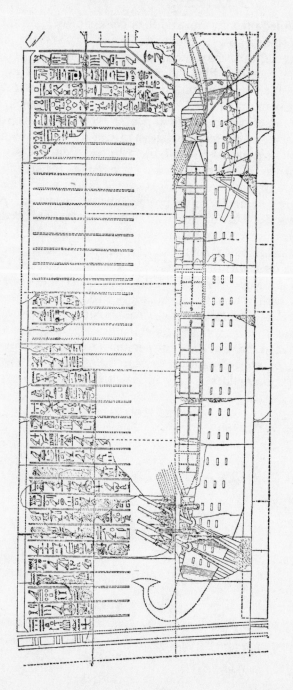

*Barge carrying two obelisks*

sand-filled pit with the sand then being slowly removed from the bottom until each monument could be manoeuvred on to its base. But we have no direct accounts of this.

The obelisks, like the pyramids, were made by men. These men left records, both written and in their works, of many of the methods they used. It took many men, much time and effort, and a great deal of wealth. We are so used to machines we forget what man can do on his own. The Egyptian pyramids were built with techniques that we can see in use in many other buildings belonging to the same period. No unusual powers were needed to build them, nor do they embody unexpected measurements or super-accuracy. Although there are only about two hundred years between the earliest pyramids and the smooth-sided, beautifully made Great Pyramid of Cheops, we can trace and date a clear line of pyramid development. The earliest pyramids are step pyramids, which have many similarities with even earlier tombs and buildings. The step pyramids use only small blocks of stone, since architects who were familiar only with mud brick were unwilling to commit themselves too far with the new medium. It is only after a generation or two of experience that the giant stone pyramids with smooth sides appear in Egyptian history.

# 5. The Likeness of Gods?

In a cave near the isolated Delemere homestead in the Northern Territory of Australia are the pictures of two giant men. One is twelve feet (four metres) tall, the other rather over six feet (about 2·2 metres). Both are dressed in tight-fitting suits with zipper-like fastenings down and across their bodies. Both are wearing heavy boots on their feet, and their hands are concealed in mitten-like gloves formed in one piece with their suits. The smaller figure wears a round helmet with goggles and has short antennae (or ears?) projecting above his head. Under his left arm he carries a weapon which looks like a one-man bazooka— an anti-tank rocket launcher. The larger figure carries no weapon, but above his face mask there rises a clear dome with above it a grid of radiating wires; it reminds us of nothing so much as an advanced one-man radar set. Perhaps he is the target-finder for the man with the weapon?

The Northern Territory has never been fought over by men with modern weapons. No American or Russian cosmonauts have landed there by mistake, to be seen and painted by any of the Aborigines. These paintings then must surely be very old, pictures of astronauts who landed on earth in prehistoric times and who so impressed the local people that their visit was recorded indelibly in paint, perhaps in larger than life size. This interpretation is certainly a logical and possible one. The figures look to us iike astronauts, in space-suits, with modern weapons. But are they?

F

In 1956 W. Arndt went to Delemere and interviewed the elders of the Wardaman tribe, on whose territory the cave is situated and to whom the "Lightning Brothers" belong. He checked ihe information with a number of Aboriginal people and also interviewed the same people again after a lapse of several years. The stories he got from different people and at different times were consistent.

The Lightning Brothers of Delemere were painted over a period of about fifteen years by an elder known as Emu Jack. In earlier times some of the Wardaman people had been able to visit another cave on Victoria River where the Lightning Brothers had originally been painted, but when white pastoralists took over most of the country early this century such visits became impractical. The elders of the tribe decided that the Brothers must move closer to Delemere so that the younger generation could see them as well as learn the traditions associated with them. Emu Jack "dreamed" the design and painted it as his time permitted. Other elders took an active part in the discussion of the design and were influential in deciding on particular aspects of the picture.

Every feature of the painting has a meaning and the painting as a whole has a complex story attached to it. The two men are tribal brothers in dispute over a woman. The smaller man is married to the woman, while the larger is a handsome young man who pays court to her. The two fight, the smaller one using a very strong stone axe, which is drawn in the traditional carrying position for axes, under his left arm.

The larger brother, Yagdjadbula, is not only taller, he has an elaborate headdress and a longer penis. The headdress is black and white like a thundercloud to indicate its strength, but the design is also based on the turbans worn by Afghan camel-drivers who were well known in the district fifty to a hundred years ago. The headdress is also sexually attractive, as is the longer penis.

The smaller brother, Tjabuindji, has no headdress and a shorter penis: he is therefore less sexually attractive. But his feet and ankles are large and blocky, so that when he stamped while warming up for the fight he made thunder. Since he was the offended party and furious, he made most of the thunder and must therefore have had very large and strong feet and ankles. So Tjabuindji's feet are larger than Yagdjadbula's.

The use of black for colouring certain lines and features such as ears, eyes, arm bindings and armpits was intended to show that these features were "strong" in a very broad sense of the term. Black is the colour of strength. So the eyes and the ears were "strong" enough to withstand the intense lightning flashes and thunder created by the fight. The armpits are black because they produced a strong body odour, common in hot, "sweaty", thundery weather. The black "zipper-fastenings" down and across the body represent the backbone and loins. Both are joined to the penis, for high sexual activity demands a strong backbone and loins, and clearly both brothers were highly sexed to stage such a furious fight over a woman.

The one feature that remains unexplained is why Emu Jack chose to portray the brothers with round mouthless faces and no necks. There is no answer to this in the research accounts of Arndt and others. So perhaps Emu Jack was visited by a couple of astronauts in the Northern Territory of Australia some time before 1930? Possible, but a little unlikely, isn't it? Why should he conceal their visit, anyway?

It becomes more unlikely when we look at other representations of humans in the region. *None* of them are completely, photographically true to life. Proportions vary, some are stick figures, others have enlarged sexual organs. A great many are highly stylized; they are more like our newspaper caricatures than like photographs. When we see a cartoon of Nixon, Mao, or Whitlam we know he does not look like that; we know that the artist has exaggerated certain features in order that we should instantly recognize the person portrayed. The same can be true of Aboriginal artists.

Not only did Aboriginal artists concentrate on certain features, they had a story to tell. In the case of the Lightning

Brothers it was a drama of sex and violence between men, so the sexual and violent parts of the men involved were stressed and other aspects of their bodies and activities ignored or played down. There are many other examples of this.

Also in the Northern Territory, for instance, we can find many pictures of human figures with heavily barbed spear-heads sticking into elbows, shoulders, knees and other joints. These figures are usually male, but females are also known. The heads are frequently little more than a featureless mask, while the sexual organs are exaggerated. These paintings occur in caves and on pieces of bark. They are sorcery paintings. If a man or woman has illicit sexual relations, the offended spouse or a relative will try to work magic on them, causing their joints to become as if barbed spears had been stuck into them, so that they will eventually die. The important features are thus the joints and the sexual organs, and it is these that are stressed in the paintings; other, less important features are ignored or played down.

What of the Wandjina figures, those enigmatic mouthless faces from north-west Australia? Are they really beings in space helmets?

The Wandjina figures are certainly humanoid figures. Many of them have arms, legs, toes and fingers and genitals. Males and females are both depicted, often together in the various sites. As far as bodies are concerned, they are little different from any other paintings of humans. The heads, however, are different. They are oval or rounded and outlined with a red band like a halo. Sometimes the red band has a series of short, fine rays projecting from it, while in other cases a more elaborate structure of rays and semicircles is depicted. The only features are a pair of eyes and a vertical squared-off nose; neither mouth nor ears are indicated. The whiteness of the head is always continued down to the level of the armpits, giving the appearance of shoulders either bare like the face or covered with a one-piece garment. Below this the bodies are usually painted with lines and dots in patterns. Not all the paintings have bodies; some have only a head and shoulders. Where there are a number of Wandjinas in the same cave there are usually a few with full bodies and many who are just heads.

How can we interpret these paintings? The Worora, in whose territory the Wandjinas are found, talk of them as a previous population of semi-mythical semi-humans. At some time in the past the Wandjinas and the Aborigines had a great fight and many people were killed. The Wandjinas then dispersed and had further individual adventures and fights, mostly with each other. But at some point each one entered a cave or shelter and transformed itself into the painting we see today. Note that the Wandjinas do not create the pictures, they actually *become* them, though their spirits may also appear simultaneously in other forms, for example in cloud formations.

The Worora say further that their responsibility to these paintings is to keep them fresh and to repaint them frequently, because if they fade and disappear so will the fertility of the countryside. They deny emphatically that they ever actually created the paintings or that they alter their characteristics.

If this is so, and if the Wandjina figures are accurate portraits of men in space helmets, how do we explain the fact that many of the figures have not only eyes, but red eyelashes? The red "halo"—it is always red—looks very much the same as the band of red ochre the Worora men paint over the front part of the top of their heads and down the sides of their faces. This headband is decorated with white dots, and so is the halo of the Wandjina figure. Behind the band the man's hair sticks up, looking like a series of small rays.

There is also one record of a Wandjina actually being painted by Aborigines. This occurred in 1929 at Langgi, and the figure is a completely new one which covers earlier Wandjina figures. It differs slightly in style from these earlier paintings at the same site. The hair is shown as a radiating network, with club-like protuberances. The nose is painted as a separate object, not joined by some lines to the edges of the forehead band as in the earlier works.

The halo itself is less thick and prominent, while more attention is given to the hair. While these changes are relatively minor, they prove that changes *can* occur in the art of painting Wandjinas.

How old are the Wandjinas? We have no definite dates for the Wandjina pictures still present in the Kimberleys. What is clear is that without continuous freshening-up, repainting and care they decay rapidly. I. M. Crawford, who has worked in this area, can show by comparing photographs taken in 1901 with the paintings as they are at present that considerable decay has occurred in many of them. They are not, of course, now being repainted with the same regularity as in the past. The extent of the damage varies directly with the degree to which the paintings are exposed to the weather, but we can estimate fairly generously that none of those now visible are likely to be older than several hundred years. If our modern example is any guide—and why shouldn't it be?—it seems likely that there have been a number of stylistic changes in Wandjinas over that period of time.

Wandjina figures are not the only rock paintings to be found in this area of Australia. There are other human figures, large numbers of snakes and many other animals, including crocodiles, dingoes, lizards and kangaroos. Several aspects of these paintings bear strong stylistic similarities to the Wandjinas and confirm that all were painted according to the same traditions.

For a start, none of the figures is highly realistic. We can recognize a kangaroo by its stance and leg proportions, a crocodile by its snout and long tail, dingoes by their head shapes, proportions and curly tails. But apart from these essential features, they are not accurate, anatomically correct drawings. There is enough to identify them and no more, and in this they resemble the Wandjina figures.

It is also noticeable that there is a conventional way of depicting the face on all the animals. Although many are apparently drawn side-on, in profile, both eyes are always shown, side by side, and the mouth line runs from the muzzle up to between the eyes. In other words, once the body and skull outline had been drawn there was a standard method of drawing a face—two dots separated by a line. This is very similar to the way of drawing Wandjina faces, so perhaps we may think that the absence of mouth on their portraits was not because they were wearing space helmets, but rather that, since they were not Aborigines, they must be drawn in the same way as all other creatures.

Further similarities are to be found in the treatment of the bodies. In nearly all cases, animal bodies are covered with rows of dots and lines, while in some cases the limbs are marked off by bands in the same way as the limbs of Wandjina figures.

If we look then at the Wandjina figures in the context of the art of the area it becomes clear that although they are strikingly dramatic figures they were none the less painted by local Aborigines, that they are not photographic representations but are subject to changes, and, most importantly, they have many similarities to paintings of other creatures found in the region. Thus they are not portrayals of ancient visitors but are painted according to a conventional Aboriginal style of depicting living creatures. To call them "spacemen" is about as true as saying that Donald Duck is drawn as a shooter's guide to duck-hunting.

In Australia there are examples, though scarce and little known, of rock paintings made by living Aborigines, who were working from an on-going tradition and not from some extra-terrestrial model. But it is clear that the only way we can be absolutely certain of finding out the meaning of any art is to ask the artists. We can certainly look at any pictures and make guesses about them, but there is no way of telling whether these are correct or not. So when we are dealing with prehistoric rock paintings we must at all times use analogies with modern tribal artists. This of course has its dangers: analogical reasoning assumes that because things seem similar in some features, they are similar in some other or in all features. Some poisonous toadstools look like mushrooms, but it would be a dangerous use of analogy to assume that you could eat them all! On the other hand, analogy has its uses. If we look at the various reasons given by modern tribal artists for painting on rocks this will give us some idea of the *possible* reasons behind prehistoric rock art. Unfortunately, not a great deal of work of this kind has been done—though W. Arndt's information about the Lightning Brothers is an example— and it is difficult to find good studies of the few remaining rock painters. Eric Ten Raa, however, has supplied detailed information about rock art among the Sandawe, a group of hunters and herdsmen who live in Tanzania, Central Africa.

There are many paintings in Sandawe country and they portray mostly animals and men with round heads like space helmets.

a                                        b

*Rock paintings from the Sandawe*

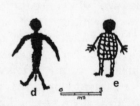

c

Both kinds of figures are still painted by the Sandawe on occasions and they recognize three main reasons why people paint. First, and least significant, is children's art. Children playing often copy rock paintings—not usually very carefully—and nowadays they also draw pictures of their teachers and other people in their society. At one place there are even a few caricatures of an archaeologist who inquired about rock art!

The second reason for painting is to help a hunter. Ten Raa met a young man drawing pictures of kudu (a kind of antelope) and was told by him that kudu had much good meat on them and that some of these animals had been sighted at Songaa, a few miles away. The next day the man went away hunting but failed to get any kudu. Not only had he been unlucky, he said, but his drawings had not been very good anyway! Hunting-magic paintings, however, are not of great significance to the Sandawe. Their making is a small ritual, along with a spell, which may help the situation but which is certainly so commonplace as to go practically unnoticed. We might well compare it to a Catholic Christian's crossing himself.

The third reason for painting is to record and prolong sacrifices which are made to clan spirits living in crevices and under boulders on hillsides well away from houses. The Sandawe pray to their spirits and seek their co-operation in promoting rainfall and keeping living people healthy. They also offer the spirits the lives of domestic animals, and as visible proof they sprinkle the blood and stomach contents of the animals on the rocks near where the spirits live. But these records will disappear quickly and sometimes the Sandawe feel that the spirits need a more lasting reminder of what has been done for them. In this case the leader of the ritual will draw a picture of the animal on the rock wall of the site and may even add an image of himself to make it quite clear to the spirits that they should be grateful to him and his clansmen.

Paintings may be made for several other reasons. A few, for example, clearly portray a dancer in the *simbo* fertility cult and may have been made to record a successful ritual. Other human paintings are made when an unusual birth, such as twins or a breech, occurs. Then the newborn child is painted as a grown person so that it may grow up strong and healthy like the picture. These paintings may also be made on special ritual wooden shields, as were those marked (d) and (e). Another reason for painting is to record unusual happenings, such as the arrival of German soldiers to "pacify" Sandawe country, but in these cases there is probably some idea of hunting magic present as well—if we paint the invaders we shall be able to hunt them better!

Many Sandawe paintings undoubtedly disappear quite quickly, being exposed to the weather. Others may last for a few hundred years, but this would be fairly rare, since none of them are painted in a completely sheltered cave.

More important, however, is the fact that Sandawe paint on rocks for a variety of purposes and they do so in a way which is not entirely photographic. The animal figure in the first picture (a) is a steer, that in the second (b) an elephant and that in the third (c) a giraffe: all are recognizable but not very precisely drawn. The same is true of the human figures, some of which are more explicit than others; but none of them are photographic and all of them use certain stylistic conventions.

No such direct information as we have for the Sandawe is available for rock paintings from most other parts of the world. There is some information about the Bushman rock art of South Africa, highly naturalistic, superbly executed in several colours—and featuring not a spaceman among the lot! But for the rest of the world, the artists practised their painting well before literate observers arrived on the scene to ask what they were doing and what their art meant. In these situations we can only assess what went on by studying the range of art produced in any area and by using analogical reasoning. One thing we cannot do, if we are to reach any valid conclusion, is pull out one or two pictures and study them in isolation. That is picking the answer you want before you ask the question. If one really wants to say that a few particular paintings are accurate representations of something unusual, then it must be shown first that they *are* unusual, second that they are accurate, and third that this is an *intended* result, not merely the outcome of a particular artistic tradition which produced pictures that *we* happen to think are like something else. If we are looking for spacemen, for example, we should find that they are clearly different from other human figures; we should also expect them to look pretty much the same all over the world. After all, the Russian and American astronauts look very similar to each other, and we might assume that the same would be true of any more advanced beings who may have visited us. They would have really perfected their space-suits by this time. What can we get from some of the prehistoric art?

In the Central Sahara, the great rock massifs of Tassili are covered with paintings. They range from completely naturalistic—vivid, alive pictures of cattle and humans—to strange distortions of reality. Among the latter there is a giant figure with a round head from which one eye peers, a few representations of a humanoid from whose head protrude five or six horns, and two beings standing like Western sheriffs about to draw their guns, but with long mask-like faces, slit ears and down-turned mouths. Taken alone, these appear strange, even freaky.

But let us look more closely not only at the few selected figures but at the total range of the art of Tassili. Jebbaren is one area within Tassili, a quarter-mile square of rock shelters with over five thousand paintings, one of which is the "Great Martian God", eighteen feet (5·5 metres) high. Along with the "Martian" are other round-headed figures. Most of the figures associated with the god are clearly naked, or nearly so, and in many of them the breasts and genitals indicate that they are women. In the same area are many other round-headed figures. Some of them carry bows and arrows and one is even shooting at another person. Some can be distinguished as male or female, while others are more economically drawn stick-like figures wearing waist-belts. One frieze of round-headed people wear horns on their heads: they might be antennae, but perhaps they are headdresses?

Near one of the giant six-horned figures at Sefar there are a considerable number of smaller, round-headed females, some of whom have two eyes, some one, some none, while at least one has a mouth as well as an eye. In one procession of more than eight women, two are clearly carrying baskets on their heads. Where the round-headed women are close to a larger creature, whether horned or round-headed, the larger one is male, often exaggeratedly so. The horned beings have no features at all; their faces are a blank. Could they be men in masks?

In addition to the "round heads" there are other, clearly human forms in which only the face has been changed. Some of them appear to have animal and bird heads, some are quite clearly wearing headdresses. There are some that have well-proportioned bodies but only tiny, stick-like heads. Every variation of style from almost surrealist to nearly natural can be found.

The same range occurs in animal representations. Some animals, especially cattle, are drawn with great care as if it were important to get all the markings right. This might be necessary if the paintings were about particular cattle— if the painter was illustrating *his* cattle and no others. And we know from many tribes in Africa today that each owner can describe exactly the markings on every cow he owns, even though his herd may contain several dozen beasts.

In contrast to this, there are animals that we can recognize only by their general outline, whose proportions are distorted and colours quite inaccurate. There are elephants with tiny heads and three legs, ostriches with bodies ten times as large as their necks, and galloping horses with legs stretched out straight in front and behind like an eighteenth-century English drawing.

There are fantastic animals, too, one with an antelope's head on an elephant's body. Did all these really exist? Most of us would say they did not, they were fanciful creatures, drawn for certain purposes now unknown, drawn by people who were not interested in photographic accuracy but in something they, their clansmen, or the spirits could recognize. If this is so for animals, could it also be true for humans?

In fact, among the "human" paintings the range from natural to stylized may be no greater than it is with animals, but we are better acquainted with humans and so we notice strange aspects among the human drawings more quickly than among the animals. That is, the variations in the drawings of humans at Tassili are no greater than those within each animal form: we notice them more readily, that's all.

The painters of Tassili, whose work almost certainly covers a period of several thousand years, were not photographers but artists. They worked within a series of stylistic conventions, stressing what was important to them and ignoring other details. We do the same if we draw a motorcar—the sillhouette of bonnet and trunk, two wheels, and most of us are satisfied that we have drawn a car our fellow-men can recognize; that is our stylistic convention. The Tassili painters had theirs also. Their "spacemen" come in a wide variety of human forms; they do not look like anyone else's "spacemen"—like Wandjinas or the Lightning Brothers or even like rock paintings from Egypt, Central Africa or Spain. Why are the Tassili spacemen different? Could they be humans in particular sorts of dress, masks and the like, portrayed in the performance of dances and ceremonies? Some of them we cannot understand. Is that so strange?

On the other side of the Mediterranean from Tassili, in northern Italy, lies Val Camonica, where the rocks are covered with hundreds, even thousands of small engravings. Some of them are of humanoid figures whose heads are encircled with a line from which rays project. But what is their context? They are found in association with hundreds of other carvings of men who do not have headdresses, but there is no other distinction in terms of shape or size. If we look at what the men with rays round their heads are doing, it is clear that they are doing much the same things as other men. Some brandish spears and possibly shields, at least one is riding what looks suspiciously like a horse. Other carvings in the same region show many scenes of everyday life, a man hammering on an anvil, two horses— or bullocks?—pulling a cart with wheels, men fighting and hunting.

Further, intensive archaeological excavations in the area have revealed only a quite ordinary prehistoric settlement, ranging in time from perhaps 3000 B.C. to the Roman Conquest in 16 B.C. The buildings of several periods, along with stone and metal tools, broken pots, remains of moulds for metal casting, animal bones and all the other debris of everyday life, have been found in close proximity to the engravings. There are no signs that any other than ordinary farmers lived there, recording their exploits on the local rocks. Many people wear headdresses, Afro-type haircuts and the like. Why not the inhabitants of Val Camonica?

If we look at the art of any region we are left with questions. Do all of us always understand our own art today? How many of us can interpret Picasso or Salvador Dali? What do any of us make of the giant mural on a building in Kings Cross, Sydney, which looks vaguely like a human face and which bears the text "Qet catpiuscm zap rupetnd daepigat". This text is in no known earthly language, and the picture is also mysterious. But would we say that this must be the work of astronauts?

Every group of people works within an established tradition and convention. Conventions differ from one group to another, and there is no known collection of rock art which was made by prehistoric photographers. The Wandjinas, "Martians", and beings with rays round their heads meant one thing to their makers, but may easily convey quite a different message to us.

# 6. Astronomers, Astronauts and Airstrips in Antiquity

In the desert plains and hills of southern Peru life is hard. The villages cling to the coast and the few narrow river valleys where water from the western Andes flows for only a few months a year. The population is now only a few thousand, living mostly by farming, fishing, and selling art to the occasional tourist driving down the Pan-American Highway. The coastal area around Nazca, in southern Peru, has none the less been settled for thousands of years, largely because of the rich fish and shellfish resources. Excavations in coastal villages show that people have been there since at least 2500 B.C. and for thousands of years before that hunters and gatherers roamed the region.

Away from the villages and gardens of today, on the dry, completely bare desert plateaux and ridges that rise between the fertile valleys and run from the ocean to the foot of the Andes, we find thousands of lines drawn on the ground. Over an area roughly sixty miles long and several miles wide, between the Palpa and Ingenio Rivers, the lines cover the ground in an extraordinary maze of conflicting shapes and directions. Most of the lines are straight; some of them go for miles, though the majority are shorter. Many are on flat ground, while others rise up hill slopes before stopping. There is always some point *on the ground*, however, from which the whole of any one line can be observed; there are none with parts hidden in valleys or behind ridges. As well as the lines, there are geometrical figures such as long thin triangles and rectangles, and a few faint animal drawings, including a bird four hundred feet (120 metres) long, a spider, a monkey and other, apparently more mythical, creatures. Many of the lines and drawings occur one above the other, intersecting at odd angles and cutting into each other, thus demonstrating that there was no one great master plan for the whole area.

All of these thousands of lines and figures are made in the same simple way, namely by moving aside some of the darker-coloured surface stones and exposing the lighter ground beneath. This was possibly because in the Peruvian desert, as in some other deserts, wind erosion has gradually removed the soil until now the ground is a veritable stone carpet, darkened on the upper side by exposure to wind and sun over millions of years. If any stone is moved, or even turned over, a patch lighter in colour than the surrounding desert is produced.

With the Nazca lines and figures, the stones that were moved to produce them are piled up at the edges so that each line or exposed area consists of a slightly lower patch of earth (the figure) surrounded by a very low ridge of stones. These ridges are often no more than a few centimetres high and are best seen in the early morning or late afternoon when the shadows are longest.

It is quite certain that the lines and other symbols are not "roads" in any normal sense, since they go from nowhere to nowhere and there are just too many of them in this small area of desert. Ever since the lines were discovered no one who has studied them has claimed that they are roads. We may be equally certain that these mysterious markings are not irrigation canals, since they are too shallow and do not join up with streams or any other sources of water. The idea that they are airstrips or an airport is equally silly. Some lines are only a few metres long, others go along rough ground and up hills. Every one of the lines is made simply by moving aside a few stones to expose the ground underneath—strong enough to take an emergency landing by an occasional Cessna perhaps, but hardly the regular landings of heavy aircraft or spacecraft. Further, what would an airport be doing with pictures of spirals, birds and animals on it?

If the lines were the remains of an aerodrome, there would surely be some other remains. Where are the foundations of the control centre? Where the dropped bolts, spanners, odd bits of junk, thrown-away food wrappings, and all the other litter that industrial technologies produce? None of these nor any other similar material has ever been found, despite much careful archaeological survey work in the area over the last thirty years. And archaeologists, who are specialists in prehistoric garbage, would certainly have found any that existed. Surely this was the cleanest airport in the world's history!

What else could these lines be?

Over the last thirty years many of the lines have been mapped by Maria Reiche and studied by her and other archaeologists. It is definitely established that a large number of them can be traced back to a dozen or more origin points. That is, the lines do not form random patterns. Rather, a person standing at one of these points can see lines and cleared areas radiating away from him in many directions. If you stand at one of the points, many of the lines can be seen to have a definite astronomical significance. Some point to the places where the sun rises and sets at the solstices (the longest and shortest days of the year) and the equinoxes (the days midway between the solstices when day and night are of equal length): these lines and others like them are easy to decipher. Others are more difficult, having no immediately obvious astronomical reference point, but it seems quite likely that they point to positions of stars or planets which the builders of the lines regarded as important.

All the "origin points" so far recorded occur on little hillocks or even artificial piles of stones, from which the radiating lines can be seen quite clearly. These points are thus in the nature of observatories, places where the move-

G

ments of sun, moon and stars could be recorded precisely, and the lines then drawn accurately.

Lines are also found associated with the cleared triangular and rectangular areas. These lines may be star-oriented, but the rising and setting positions of the stars have changed so considerably over the last few thousand years, owing to the earth's movement within the galaxy, that this is difficult to confirm. But it is not impossible: astronomers and mathematicians are able to calculate the past apparent movement of the stars and predict (or rather, retrodict) where they would have risen at any particular time in the past. This aspect of the Nazca lines is being studied at present. One obvious candidate for inclusion, for example, is the Great Bear (Ursa Major) constellation which is visible at Nazca in November and whose appearance coincides with the annual flood season and the beginning of the agricultural year.

The rectangular and triangular cleared areas themselves generally have, like the origin points, a large stone heap at one or both ends from which all the lines that leave the area can be seen. Presumably these heaps are also observation points, and the cleared areas may have served as temples or sacred meeting-places of some kind.

Not all lines, however, relate to astronomical observations. In at least one case a line marks the position on the ground of the edge of the shadow of a large hill at the time of the winter solstice. We may guess that other important, but equally obscure, observations occur also.

As well as lines, the Nazca plains also contain a series of huge "drawings"—one of them five hundred feet (150 metres) long. They are made in the same way as the other markings, by moving stones aside and exposing lighter-coloured ground beneath. One peculiar feature is that each picture is drawn in an uninterrupted line or path, which begins at one point and twists and turns until the design is completed, without ever crossing itself. This is characteristic of processional paths in many religious ceremonials—including some Christian ritual—and may indicate that the "drawings" were intended for use during religious observances. In at least one case a drawing is the continuation of a long straight solstice line, thus linking that figure with astronomical observations. All the figures, moreover, are associated with a large enclosure or wide line like a road, thus confirming their part in the overall complex structure.

The drawings are not only of animals—spider, bird, monkey, serpents—but of plants and geometric designs, including spirals. Their general appearance is similar to that of designs found on pottery and textiles in prehistoric Nazca villages of about A.D. 600, by radiocarbon dating. Interestingly, a wooden post found at the intersection of two of the Nazca lines has also been dated to about A.D. 500-600, thus confirming that the lines were being used at that time.

We have no definite information about the mechanical aids that may have been used in making these giant drawings. Probably the makers first drew a rectangular grid over their original small design and then used a larger replica of the same grid to help them trace the large design on the desert. Faint remains of what appear to be such rectilinear guide-lines have been found near some of the figures.

Apart from the lines that can be linked to the sun and moon, there are a number of lines and "roads" that we cannot directly link to any astronomical observation. What can these be? Paul Kosok and Maria Reiche, who have done most of the mapping and interpretation of these lines, make several suggestions.

1. The lines could refer to rising and setting of the sun and moon on other important days of the Nazcans' year.

2. They could relate to the rising and setting of certain planets or stars, which we know were important for religious purposes in many parts of Central and South America.

3. They may serve to link two sight lines, or points, or figures that the Nazcans decided were particularly important. This, of course, would be extremely difficult to decipher.

Are the Nazca lines unique? Clearly, they have been extraordinarily well preserved in the desert environment, which no one wanted for any economic purpose and in which no figure was ever destroyed by rain, storms, or soil erosion. So they are better preserved than most other examples. But farther south in Peru, in the smaller, poorer valleys near the Chilean border, there are similar markings, though they are smaller and fewer in number than those around Nazca.

There are two ways we can look at these lines. The first is to see them as part of the same system as other giant figures and even sand drawings found in many parts of the world. Some of these are astronomical, others are not, but all are using the ground as a canvas on which to sketch important observations relevant to aspects of religious or everyday life.

The other approach is to see the lines as a kind of architecture, the monumental record of some ritual activity. It is two-dimensional, unlike the three-dimensional massive buildings that we think of as public architecture, and it is consecrated, as George Kubler says, to human *actions* rather than to shelter.

Have we any proof that the lines were made by the pre-historic ancestors of the present people? Direct proof, no, but what would we need? An inscription that said so? That we do not have, but there are several reasons for believing that the Nazcans, and no other people, made and used these "lines".

First, there is the similarity between the desert drawings and the designs on Nazca pottery and textiles dated to about A.D. 500. Then there is the fact that only this pottery and other material from that period has been found over the entire area. Not one piece of material that would be out of place in that society has ever been found over the entire area of the Nazca lines or in near-by settlements. Further, like many other American groups, the Nazcans probably had a strong belief in astrology—in the power of heavenly bodies to influence earthly events—and would have made appropriate astronomical observations. These would have been helpful in planning such matters as when to plant crops and perform ceremonies also. As one of the early Spanish chroniclers wrote, "These Indians watched the heavens and the signs very constantly, which made them such great soothsayers." Finally, the simple fact that so many of the lines *are* astronomically oriented makes it likely that prehistoric Nazcans and not astronauts were the makers. Why would people who could fly to the stars bother to move a few desert stones in order to point to the sunrise?

The final question which might be asked is how much we know about the history of man in the Nazca valley, and whether it differs notably from the history of other Peruvian valleys.

The Nazca valley is one of a number that drain the Andes through the dry Peruvian desert to the Pacific coast. As in the other valleys, the first towns developed out of farming communities about two thousand years ago, but the city which then grew up at Cahuachi also contained a temple pyramid like many other cities farther north and in the highlands. At the same time major irrigation systems were constructed to control nearly all the water in the valley, and the presence of these systems almost certainly points to some valley-wide central political authority which would be responsible for their annual cleaning and the distribution of water to all farmers. About A.D. 500 population pressure on scarce land and resources caused war and conquest to become endemic in coastal Peru, and the people of Nazca conquered those of the next valley, Acari.

Nazca society of this time is famous for the beauty and elegance of its art work; the pottery bottles and bowls and textiles use several different colours to portray scenes of everyday life and mythology. The artists painted a wide variety of plants and animals, including monkeys which can only have been imported from the Amazonian jungles on the other side of the Andes. Among the mythological beings are men, birds, and killer whales, each usually shown with the heads of defeated enemies collected as trophies and the semicircular knives used for cutting them off. The picture of valley life at this time has been described by Ed Lanning as one of "an intensely specialized and stratified society with well-defined ranks and professions symbolized by details of dress and ornament".

This society reached its most highly developed form about A.D. 500, and it was then that its people constructed the elaborate, astronomically oriented "Nazca lines" in the desert near their home.

In addition to these lines, there is also the great trident figure on the hillside above the Bay of Pisco, 125 miles (200 kilometres) west-north-west of Nazca. The figure is 128 metres long and 74 metres wide and is on a steep mountain slope of 42 degrees. It is excavated through a thin sand layer into a hard, white, stony salt crust that lies on top of red bedrock in this region. That is to say it is not made out of stone blocks, but simply dug into the white ground; it gleams with the whiteness of pure salt, not phosphorescence.

The figure appears to represent a tree with a trunk and three branches, on which leaves and flowers can be seen. Three-branched trees are frequent in Peruvian textile designs and are often symbolic of the arrival of good fortune.

Today the figure is believed by local people to be a Christian monument and there is even a legend that it was made by a nun. Every year, therefore, there is a pilgrimage to keep it clean and free from drifting sand. Local believers, not some mysterious forces, keep it shining in the sunlight.

We do not know why the Pisco tree or trident was made, or even when, since no other archaeological material has been found with it. But the fact that the design is like that on locally woven and embroidered textiles dated between A.D. 1 and A.D. 1000 suggests that it comes from this period and may have some religious function.

Single giant figures cut into the ground and astronomical observations are not, of course, a monopoly of the ancient Peruvians. In the northern part of the United States there are mounds built in animal shapes, while sand and dirt drawings occur in many parts of the world. In England there are such figures as the White Horse of Uffington, the Cerne giant and many others.

The motions of the sun, moon and stars have also been used by men in many parts of the world as a guide by which to organize their lives. Stonehenge, for instance, a circle and a half of stones surrounded by a bank and ditch and with an avenue one and a half miles (2·4 kilometres) long, also banked and ditched, leading to it, is clearly related to astronomical observations. The structure is aligned roughly and approximately on the midsummer sunrise and it was clearly built with this in mind. Recent suggestions that it was an accurate observatory or a computer, however, are based on *in*accurate measurements and dubious assumptions. Alignments of stones, for instance, are accepted if they are within two degrees of the right direction. This is about twenty-four times the error incurred experimentally simply by using a pair of sticks as sighting guides. In other words, by using a pair of straight sticks and other simple equipment far greater accuracy could have been achieved than by using the stones. If Stonehenge was a high-powered computer or observatory the results must have been extraordinarily inaccurate.

In more recent times, Christian temples and churches have commonly been built in a cross-shape, visible to some extent from the ground but much more clearly directed towards a god thought of as "up there", viewing us from the sky.

When men make designs that are best seen from the sky or take an interest in the stars it does not prove that there are astronauts. It proves that most people believe that gods are "up there" rather than down below us underground (though such beliefs are also known), or in the same world as we are but in some distant place.

The Nazca lines and the Pisco trident, like Stonehenge, the White Horse, and Westminster Cathedral demonstrate man's faith in the gods, be they single, male and Christian or multiple and heavenly bodies—the sun, moon and stars. All must be worshipped in appropriate ways.

## THE PIRI RE'IS MAP

Almost a thousand years after the Nazcans drew their lines in the Peruvian desert, a Turkish admiral and geographer called Piri Re'is put the finishing touches to his map of the world. Drawn on a gazelle skin, it was a world chart on a large scale, intended to summarize all the information available to him in A.D. 1513 in Gallipoli, Turkey.

Today we have only a fragment of his map—the fragment representing the Atlantic Ocean, the Americas and the western edges of Europe and Africa. The rest has been torn off and lost during the last four centuries. It is this fragment which is claimed to be so accurate that it must have been drawn from satellite photographs or a high-flying aircraft. This same fragment is also supposed to show the coasts of Antarctica so correctly that they must have been mapped at a time when the continent was free from ice. Is this indeed the case? Do we have a sixteenth-century map which is drawn from photographs taken above Cairo? Let us first hear from Piri Re'is himself, writing a note in Turkish on the margin of his own map:

> This section explains the way the map was prepared. Such a map is not owned by anybody at this time. I, personally drew and prepared this map. In preparing this map I made use of about twenty old charts and eight Mappa Mundis; that is of the charts . . . prepared at the time of Alexander the Great and in which the whole inhabited world was shown; of the chart of the West Indies; and of the new maps made by four Portuguese containing the Indian and Chinese countries geometrically represented on them. I also studied the chart that Columbus drew for the West. Putting all these materials together in a common scale I produced the present map.*

Several things stand out quite clearly from this statement. First, Piri Re'is was not producing an original map of the world but was putting one together on the basis of existing knowledge. Being a subject of the Ottoman Empire, when he drew various maps together on a common scale he centred them on a convenient local geographical point— not actually Cairo, but the junction between the Tropic of Cancer and the longitude of Alexandria. Alexandria was the most famous ancient town for mariners, and the one that had been used as one reference point by all Greek

---

* C. Hapgood, *Maps of the Ancient Sea Kings*, p. 217.

geographers, including those who made the type of maps (known as *mappa mundi*) which Piri Re'is used. Everyone who was likely to use his map knew where Alexandria was, and to combine its longitude with the Tropic of Cancer meant his map used a basic reference point which could be widely understood.

In making his map this way Piri Re'is was thus conforming to the accepted standards of his time. Maps drawn in the fourteenth and fifteenth centuries used Alexandria as the reference point if they were primarily based on Greek maps, or other important towns in the Mediterranean area if they belonged to civilizations centred farther west. For example, even the Vinland map, which was drawn in northern Europe about 1440 and possibly records the Viking discovery of North America, has the Mediterranean Sea as its centre, for that was the centre of the Renaissance world.

But, it may be said, did Piri Re'is perhaps not know how accurate his map was? Was his map merely a copy of a copy of a highly accurate original taken from aerial photographs?

Piri Re'is, of course, as his own statement shows, was no mere copier. His map drew together the information from at least thirty-four others, dating from different times and drawn in different parts of the world. If his map is superaccurate, then all of these maps, his sources, would have to be as accurate as the final document. We still have some of them, and clearly this is not the case. In order to prove this, we must look more closely at the maps and geographical knowledge of the fifteenth century.

In the fifteenth century there were three main types of map available, and all of them were used by Piri Re'is. One type was the *mappa mundi*, with Jerusalem at the centre and Europe, Asia and Africa—the entire known world—fitted in around it. These maps have no scale or proportion; they were designed to illustrate Bibles and J. R. Hale calls them "a visual equivalent of Genesis". Their contribution to the Piri Re'is map was to reinforce the classical Greek idea of centring all maps somewhere in the eastern Mediterranean.

The second group of maps was based on classical Greek sources, especially the map-maker Ptolemy of Alexandria. These maps were oval or rectangular, had a fair knowledge of Asia—derived from Arab traders, the explorations of Marco Polo and others—and also depicted a great southern continent, Terra Australis, which had to be there if the world was not to be top-heavy. After all, the logical Greeks reasoned, all the land around Europe and Asia must have some counterweight! Early Ptolemaic maps show this southern continent joined on to Africa, but once Africa had been circumnavigated by the Portuguese in 1488 that was clearly wrong. Piri Re'is probably knew this, but that portion of his map has been lost. The great southern continent on his map still joins up with the Americas. This is probably because he drew it in 1513, six years before Magellan sailed round the southern tip of America, Cape Horn, and showed that the Americas and Terra Australis were also separate continents.

The third group of maps was quite different, sailors' charts of local coasts. Such charts did not worry about an overall picture of the world, but only about the coastline of a particular area, for practical men to use in their trading voyages. The one fragment of a map made by Columbus that survives today is a sketch of the north-west coast of Hispaniola, firmly in the tradition of traders', explorers' and sailors' charts. This fragment is not the one used by Piri Re'is, but the one he did use for the Americas was, as he says, drawn by Columbus, and was probably in this same tradition. To fit local charts into a world map meant they had to be reduced to a common scale and fitted into a complete picture—not an easy thing to do.

Until the European explorers started to discover the world in the late fifteenth and sixteenth centuries the many errors in these three kinds of maps were not realized. One universal error was in thinking that there was far more land than sea. The distance between Western Europe and Asian coasts, for example, was usually thought to be no more than five thousand miles—about seven thousand miles shorter than the real distance—while Columbus himself believed the distance was only three thousand five hundred miles. Before setting out on his voyages, that is, he believed that Cipango (Japan) would be found approximately in the place we know as the Caribbean. No wonder he thought he had discovered Asia and the Indies! Only when Balboa sighted the Pacific in 1513 did it become apparent that the world was much bigger than anyone thought.

So the maps that Piri Re'is used, according to his own statement, were of three kinds, all showing their authors' ideas of what the world was like, and each having various errors and distortions. Therefore they cannot have been the only sources if his map is as completely accurate as has been claimed.

Just how accurate is it, anyway?

One of the characteristics of aerial photographs is that they are extremely precise. Every mountain, lake and river-mouth is shown with impartiality. Not a mile of coast is missed, not an island inserted or overlooked. To be sure, in some parts of the world clouds obscure some features for much of the time, but the photographs will show these clouds, and an accurate map-maker will leave a gap there until clearer photographs become available. If we are to believe Piri Re'is's map is based on photographs it must be completely accurate.

Let us start with Europe, closest to the assumed satellite photographer. We may notice immediately that the centre of Spain contains a vast lake, with three rivers leading from it to the Atlantic and Mediterranean oceans. A similar network of lakes occurs in Africa, including the area now covered by the Sahara desert, and farther south to the Gold Coast. While there has certainly been a time when the climate of the Sahara was wetter, a network of lakes like that depicted should leave some traces on the ground. There are none. Nor was there ever a lake of that size in central Spain.

When we move to the Americas the distortions are considerably greater. This could be expected if Piri Re'is was using currently available geographical knowledge—twenty years after Columbus, six years before Magellan—but it is quite strange if aerial photographs were used. The distortions that are easily visible include the complete omission of both the Straits of Magellan and Drake Strait, the five hundred miles (800 kilometres) of sea between Cape Horn at the southern end of America, and Antarctica. The passage that Magellan was to sail through just six years later is not shown at all! Just south of the bulge of Brazil about a thousand miles (1,600 kilometres) of coastline have also been overlooked, thus giving the map of South America a very foreshortened appearance. Moving farther north we find the Amazon River with three mouths, one of them four hundred miles from the other two, while a number of extra, non-existent islands dot the southern Caribbean Sea and Atlantic Ocean. In the Gulf of Mexico and Caribbean area of Central America the map is far more complete, as we should expect if it drew on the explorations of Columbus and his immediate successors. But even there there is one outstanding error. On Piri Re'is's map what we know as Cuba is a large rectangular island called Espaniola. It bears a close resemblance to the island known in many maps of earlier times as Cipango. Cipango is found on maps dated well before Columbus's voyage and was known originally from Marco Polo's travels as an island lying off China. It is, of course, Japan, which was given a conventional rectangular shape by Western map-makers for so many years. Piri Re'is's Espaniola is just like Cipango in shape and is not at all like the long, thin island of Cuba, whether mapped from an Alexandria-based satellite or anywhere else. Clearly Piri Re'is thought that one of the islands Columbus discovered was Japan—as did many other Europeans at the time, including Columbus himself.

If only major errors like these occurred, one might attribute them to the inevitable errors of copyists who did not understand what they were doing. But in addition there are many less obvious errors—islands put in where none exist, peninsulas and coastline conventionally drawn rather than accurately represented, even the rough outline of an Antarctic continent that is several hundred miles in error. The fact that the Antarctic coast is a pretty ordinary-looking coast in shape—apart from the Palmer peninsula projecting towards South America—meant that almost anything ancient map-makers drew would look about right, provided they were not too fanciful. A careful comparison of the ancient maps with any modern map will at once reveal a multitude of differences between imagined and actual coastlines.

The Piri Re'is map can therefore be seen as being a very fair example of early sixteenth-century map-making. It does not record undiscovered territory and the mapping is only reasonably accurate. There are so many gross mistakes that it seems impossible to think that any satellite photographer can be involved. In addition, we can see this map as having the strengths and weaknesses of other maps drawn at the same period—it portrays the geographical knowledge of people of the time when it was drawn.

THE MAYAN CALENDAR

The Mayan calendar, like the Piri Re'is map, is claimed to possess extraordinary accuracy, this time astronomical. The Mayan Indians, whose two million descendants still live in Central America, were the founders of a great civilization in the jungles of Honduras. There, between A.D. 1 and 900 their civilization flourished, with many priests in the ritual centres such as Tikal, Copan, and Kaminaljuyu, which served and were served by the peasants of the surrounding countryside. The Mayan calendar was used as a basis for all major activities, which the priests said had to be carefully and ritually regulated in order to ensure their successful outcome.

Our knowledge of ancient Mayan thought is only a fraction of the whole, for of the thousands of written records only three accounts, all of them ritual-astronomical works, have survived the heavy hand of Catholic missionaries. These, together with the carved stone stelae, comprise our current stock of written Mayan records.

These records show that the Mayan historical thought depended on a theory that the universe continually went through cycles of creation and destruction. These cycles

were each about 5,200 years long and there were thirteen
of them in all. The end of the final one would mark the
complete destruction of the world and all degenerate people.
We do not know which of the thirteen cycles the Maya
considered they lived in, but whichever it was it began in
3113 B.C. and was to be completed on Christmas Eve,
A.D. 2011, when our present universe would be destroyed,
and hopefully a new cycle inaugurated.

We might note in passing that the working out of a
fixed date for the beginning of the world is quite a common
practice. The current Jewish calendar begins at the year
3761 B.C., and until late in the nineteenth century many
European Christians believed that the world was created
in 4004 B.C., and one enterprising cleric even deduced that
it began on 23rd October at 9 a.m. So the Mayan calendrical organization was not so very unusual.

The Maya, like the people of other Central American
civilizations, divided their 5,200-year cycle into 360-day
periods (*tun*) which were calculated in multiples of 18
and 20:

> 20 kins = 1 uinal (20 days)
> 18 uinals = 1 tun (360 days)
> 20 tun = 1 katun (7,200 days)
> 20 katun = 1 baktun (144,000 days)

and so on. Any date could thus be calculated to the exact
number of days from the beginning of this world cycle. One
would end up with a date which read 9.14.19.8.0—that is,
9 baktuns, 14 katuns, 19 tuns, 8 uinals, 0 kins, or 1,390,800
days since the beginning of the cycle.

For everyday purposes, of course, that system was un-
necessarily complex and the Maya used a Calendar Round
of fifty-two years. No one knows why this number was
chosen, but it is present in all the civilizations of Mesoamerica, not only the Mayan. The 52-year Round is made
up of two interwoven cycles—the 260-day *tzolkin* and a
365-day "year". The 260-day cycle itself consisted of inter-
meshing sets of twenty names with 13 numbers. Each day,
with its own name and number, also had its own series of

*Date carved on a
Mayan stela*

omens so that the 260-day cycle could be used as an astrological guide to action. This part of the calendar still survives in an unchanged form in Southern Mexico, where despite four centuries of Catholic rule the Mayan calendrical priests still keep account of the days according to the old 260-day cycle and advise their clients on their chances of success or misfortune. The 365-day cycle—the year— was the other component of the 52-year Round. It was

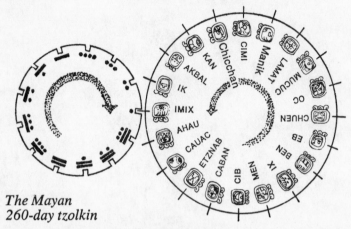

*The Mayan*
*260-day tzolkin*

based on the actual year, that is certain, but the Maya took no account of the extra quarter-day which we catch up on every four years by using 29th February. So the Mayan 365-day calendar was not, except at the beginning, directly related to the real or seasonal year. The "Vague Year", as Michael Coe calls it, consisted of 18 months of 20 days each, plus five unlucky days at the end. The myth that the Mayan year was really exact is nothing more than that— the Maya did not calculate in fractions at all, only whole numbers. So their system was quite unable to take account of the quarter-day in a 365¼-day year.

The meshing of the 260- and 365-day cycles meant that each day within the 52-year Round had a different designation, which was a combination of its name in each of the two cycles. The day represented in the part of the Calendar Round illustrated would be called 1 Kan 1 Pop. It would only occur once in each 52-year cycle. (*Illustration p. 101.*)

As well as their ordinary calendar the Maya also had a lunar calendar based on the 29-and-a-bit days between successive new moons. Actually the Maya decided that the moon months had either 29 or 30 days and calculated a correlation with the solar calendar on that basis. Over all, however, their figures were very accurate and the *average* lunar month they eventually reached was accurate to within three decimal places. But this calculation, which was

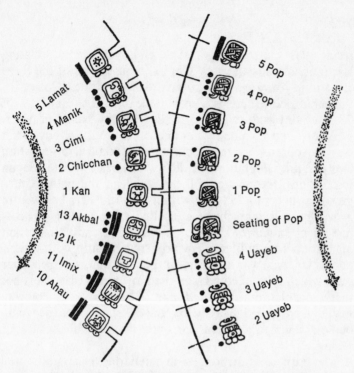

*Part of the Mayan 52-year Calendar Round*

actually that 149 moons would appear every 4,400 days, was not worked out until about A.D. 682 by the priests at one settlement, Copan, and this formula was then adopted by other centres. There is *no* evidence that the *average* lunar month was ever worked out to three decimal places by the Maya. Rather they built up a formula of whole-day months which, over a period of just over three years, kept their months in accurate alliance with the appearance of the moon. It seems likely that this lunar calendar was the one used for agricultural and other purposes for which an accurate correlation of activities with seasons was essential.

Mayan astronomers also knew that the "year" of the planet Venus was about 584 days long and that five of these "years" equalled eight Earth years of 365 days. In fact the conjunction is not quite correct, since the Venus and Earth years are 583·92 and 365·242 days respectively, but for the Maya, who worked in whole numbers, the

H

result was close enough. The eight-year table, relating Earth and Venusian years, can be found in one of the three remaining Mayan books known as the Dresden Codex. In the same book there is also a table that lists multiples of 78, probably with reference to the 780-day "year" of Mars.

Aside from fortune-telling and other ritual activity, what was the purpose of this accurate astronomical observation and careful calculation? Until we can read all the Mayan inscriptions, the answer will not be clear, but enough progress has been made to show that Mayan rulers believed in astrology and must have consulted their priests for cosmological auguries before undertaking any important action, civil or military. We need not be surprised if their particular type of astrological beliefs differed from our own, which rely, of course, on the movements of planets not really visible to the naked eye. The Mayan astrologers would have relied heavily on the most obvious heavenly bodies, since these were the ones they could be sure of seeing.

The purpose of the long-term calendrical calculation may also be understood. Each Mayan city—Tikal, Palenque, Copan and so on—was ruled over by a dynasty whose history and exploits are recorded in carvings and stelae. Part of each history refers to very ancient times, when god-like ancestors of the dynasty were supposed to have lived. A precise calculation of *when* they ruled would naturally lend conviction to the idea that they *did* rule and thus support their supposed descendants' claims to power.

The astronomical systems of the Maya were concentrated on the heavenly bodies most visible to the naked eye. They did not have telescopes, and the demonstrations of their knowledge needed to be visible to those over whom they ruled. To predict an eclipse of the sun is far more dramatic than to predict the rising of a star few others can see or care about. Their calendar system was based, certainly, on careful calculations and extended observations, but these were no more than any of us, working without telescopes, could perform if we had the conviction that this was the right way to regulate the affairs of men and gods.

# 7. Strange Buildings and Carvings

In many parts of the world today there are outstanding relics of the past. Enormous cities have been found entirely covered with jungle in Central America and south-east Asia; great stone fortifications are perched high on mountains, carvings seem to portray other-worldly beings. Who built these things, and to what design? What are the mysteries of Tiahuanaco, Palenque, Sacsahuaman and Zimbabwe? Did a rocket blast off from Chichen Itza, leaving a circular hole to become a sacred well? Who built the pyramid and stone heads in the middle of the marsh at La Venta? Were these all built by apprentices to the same master-builders? Do they embody superhuman feats? Let us look at each of these places and see how they were built, where the stones came from, when they were made and, perhaps, why they were built at all.

## SOUTH AMERICA: SACSAHUAMAN, MACHU PICCHU AND TIAHUANACO

Almost five hundred years ago, Spanish explorers arrived in Peru in search of El Dorado, the lost city of gold. They found not only gold but the Inca empire as well. From their capital, Cuzco, the Inca rulers controlled some six million people, ruling as benevolent despots in a tightly controlled regime. The whole country was organized in a paramilitary chain of command and it was common, for instance, for thousands of newly conquered peoples to be moved from their home areas and resettled so that they would have fewer local ties, and of necessity be more loyal to the empire. Inca control over Peru and northern Chile lasted less than a hundred and fifty years, but in that time the Incas built a comprehensive road network, a swift postal system, and a rapidly moving army.

The Spaniards took over this empire, killed its rulers, pillaged its wealth and built a Christian church over the main Inca palace at Cuzco. But enough of pre-Spanish Cuzco has survived to make us wonder at the immensity and fine detail of the stonework. Stone walls, some of them built of regular square blocks but others of blocks that are wildly irregular in shape and size, occur at Cuzco and Sacsahuaman, at Machu Picchu, a thousand metres above the Urubamba River, and at other towns and forts. Some of these walls are made of granite, one of the hardest and least tractable of building stones. The cities and forts where this stonework is found are often on mountain tops and almost inaccessible ridges. Why were these towns built? How were the rocks shaped and moved?

It is worth starting at Cuzco, today the most accessible of the Inca towns, and the one with the famous "stone with twelve corners", which fits perfectly with all its neighbours. How was this done? Looking at a photograph of this stone, it is clear that many of the joints between it and its neighbours are not straight, but slightly curved, and that the corners are rounded off. This is characteristic of stones ground to their final shape *on the wall itself*, each stone being adjusted to the irregularities of its neighbours. Grinding was carried out simply by rubbing the stones against each other, perhaps with some fine sand or powder between them as an abrasive. Grinding stones together, of course, often produces curved surfaces unless the techniques used are very exact. For example, the grindstones used for grains and seeds by early agriculturalists throughout the world are usually dish-shaped, with the centre part of the lower stone being worn down by the pressure of the stone above as it is pushed backwards and forwards. When larger stones are involved no one is strong enough to push down on them to grind them in this way, and it is much easier to move the stone from side to side; but in this case there is nothing to force the stones together and make the surfaces grind together and become smooth. So what was actually done was to fasten ropes over the stones and pull down on them, as well as moving the stone from side to side; this put more pressure on the edges, where the ropes pulled down, and thus made the stones grind together rather faster there, resulting eventually in a slightly convex shape for the lower stone and a slightly concave shape for the upper. This unintentionally curved shape occurs on much pre-Spanish fine stonework at Cuzco and at other Inca towns.

So we can now work out how the stone with twelve corners was formed and placed and also the order in which the stones were almost certainly laid. Notice, for instance, how stone number 4 has been worked in as a wedge under its own weight and numbers 7 and 8 fit snugly into small notches. The stones had to be laid in a certain order.

Three kinds of stone are used in the pre-Spanish buildings at Cuzco and at the hilltop fort of Sacsahuaman, only a short distance away. Two of them, limestone and diorite porphyry, are available locally and are used for over ninety per cent of the building, the porphyry being especially useful in enclosure walls where extreme solidity was necessary to hold up massive buildings. The only stone transported any distance is black andesite, which outcrops at two places 15 and 35 kilometres away. This is used only in prominent areas in the "Temple of the Sun" and other Inca palaces: it is not lavishly wasted, and was clearly a scarce resource.

Stones were moved on rollers with the aid of wooden levers and men pulling on ropes. A stone block abandoned between the andesite quarry and a building site was found early this century with wooden rollers still in place beneath it. In the Inca walls themselves we find many of the stones have small knobs left on them, clearly for the levers to work on, and some knobs show signs of this use even today. Other building stones, especially at Sacsahuaman, have indentations in similar places, and these could be used in the same way for fractional adjustments of the positioning of each block.

Blocks were raised on to walls by using an earth and rubble ramp. One of the first Spaniards to visit the Inca region saw this technique used in the building of Cuzco cathedral about A.D. 1610, while a half-finished circular stone tomb at the town of Puno still has such a ramp in place. An empire that controlled several million people could easily organize a few thousand of them, if necessary, to pull stone blocks around, especially for a ruler's palace.

Most of the shaping of stone was done with stone hammers, preferably made of haematite or other heavy ores. Hammer marks can still be seen on the limestone blocks used for building most of the walls of Sacsahuaman. Bronze and wooden crowbars were also used, and bronze chisels of several different shapes, probably for fine work, have been found.

Sacsahuaman is a fortified hilltop near Cuzco, to which the population could retreat in times of emergency. The building of such fortresses is an ancient practice in the Andes region, and Sacsahuaman is simply the most recent and most elaborately built of a series of forts, some of which date back to 1000 B.C. As in other forts, the stone walls of Sacsahuaman are set in a zigzag fashion so that defenders could always get a view of an attacker's back as well as his face and weapons. Since the fortress of Sacsahuaman was available for retreat, the Inca capital of Cuzco was not fortified.

On the north side of this fortress is a wall built of enormous blocks of local porphyry, but similar walls of much smaller blocks occur on the other sides. Inside the walls are limestone houses and the foundations of three great towers, one of which was for water storage. All the building methods and pottery at Sacsahuaman are Inca in style: there is nothing unusual there except the use of some enormous boulders for one wall. But these boulders were collected locally and were only moved into position at ground level. They occur on the lowest level of the fortifications, a straight pull from their source. The inner walls, higher up the hill, contain no such giant blocks. If the fortress was built using superhuman techniques, why were these used in such a human way?

The town of Machu Picchu is about a hundred kilometres north-west of Cuzco. It lies in a saddle between two peaks, almost surrounded by precipices dropping to the Urubamba River. The town is about seven hundred metres long and consists of many stone-walled garden terraces, which hold back the soil in small fields, and stone houses. The bases of the houses are built of large stones, the upper walls of smaller ones, sometimes well cut and squared off, but mostly just random stones set in a clay mortar. The settlement is linked together by many staircases and the houses are crowded together. Machu Picchu does not have a main defensive wall; only the area near the town gate is defended in this way. Otherwise the inhabitants relied on the precipices to keep intruders out.

Machu Picchu is only one of a number of towns of this kind along the Urubamba River. Some are high on mountain tops, others are on the narrow flood-plain of the river. Almost certainly Machu Picchu, like Pisac, Inty Pata and other mountain-top settlements, was permanently occupied by only a small number of people, but, like Sacsahuaman, served as a place of retreat in times of danger.

People who lived along the Urubamba River were on the edge of the Inca empire's control and were open to attack by wild Indians from the upper Amazon, an area which the Incas could never conquer. So like other people in other parts of the world they built a retreat for times of danger. The Acropolis at Athens, some medieval castles of Europe, and the earthen *pa* forts of the Maoris were constructed for similar reasons to Machu Picchu and Sacsahuaman.

The other mysterious city in Peruvian history is Tiahuanaco, just south of Lake Titicaca, nearly 3·8 kilometres above sea level. The main ruins cover an area of only 1,000 metres by 450 metres, and the building materials include sandstone blocks weighing up to a hundred tons. But outside this area are refuse deposits, so that clearly quite a number of people lived round the main buildings.

Today some twenty thousand people live in the well-watered pastures of the Tiahuanaco valley. They live by traditional agricultural practices, growing old crops such as potatoes in the old ways, and keeping small herds of llamas. Their patterns of life differ little from those of their ancestors, and we can therefore assume that the population of the valley has been much the same for a long time.

The major ruins at Tiahuanaco are a loose group of buildings that have been raided for their stone for at least five hundred years, so that it is difficult to discover exactly their original form. There seem to be three important buildings. Akapana is an earthen platform 210 metres square and 15 metres high, which was originally of truncated pyramidal form with a building on top of it, according to the early Spaniards who saw it before stone-robbing started. Adjacent to this is Calasasaya, a U-shaped platform 130 metres across; while about a thousand metres away Puma Puncu repeats both forms on a slightly smaller scale. All the constructions were of earth with stone facings. The simplest building technique found at Tiahuanaco consists of stone uprights like fence-posts with dry-stone walling

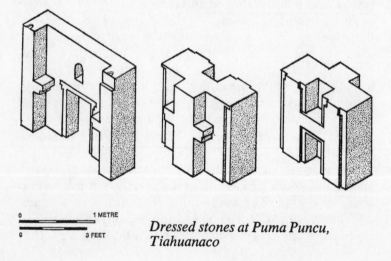

0                    1 METRE

0                    3 FEET

*Dressed stones at Puma Puncu, Tiahuanaco*

between them. Then in some better-made walls the stones are fastened together by matching T-shaped channels into which molten copper was poured to form H-shaped cramps. Finally the Puma Puncu building is littered with stone slabs cut with tongues and mortice-tenon joints so that they would slot together like woodwork. (*Illustration p. 108.*)

The site is built of sandstone and basalt blocks, with the largest sandstone ones weighing about a hundred tons. These were brought from a quarry five kilometres away, probably on wooden rollers. But, as recorded elsewhere in the world, enough men and rollers can easily move hundred-ton blocks overland.

The important thing about Tiahuanaco is that it was only a medium-sized city. There are habitation refuse deposits outside the central area, but these are not very large and it seems likely that Tiahuanaco was both a residential centre and a ceremonial centre for the surrounding valley, a very common pattern in Central and South America. Carbon dating shows that it was occupied by A.D. 300 and discoveries of Tiahuanaco-style pottery in dated sites on the Peruvian coast show that it was still operating nearly a thousand years later. When the Spaniards arrived the buildings were still almost intact, but the ceremonial aspects had been lost or destroyed during Inca rule. There is nothing to suggest the site is much more than two thousand years old.

One significant local feature of Tiahuanaco is the use of single-piece stone doorways. These are quite common in the ruins, and the most famous of them is the "Gateway of the Sun". This is carved from a single piece of andesite 3 metres high and 3·75 metres wide. The doorway was broken some time in the past but was restored and re-erected later, though its original position is unknown. On one side of the monolith, above the doorway, is a carved frieze consisting of a large human figure placed centrally with many smaller figures running towards him. The carving of the figures is just like those found on other Tiahuanaco statues and the designs are also similar to those found painted on pottery from the site.

The main figure carries rods and both these and his head-dress are decorated with puma and condor (eagle) heads. Human heads hang from his belt and he is probably weeping—at least, there seem to be tears on his cheeks. The smaller figures repeat the human-puma-condor motifs: they are winged, but some are human.

There is no evidence that links these figures to the sun. Even the name "Gateway of the Sun" is recent, given to the Tiahuanaco carving by some enterprising tourist guide: there is nothing in the carving or in Tiahuanaco to support the name.

About A.D. 600, however, objects showing the "Gateway

god", his attendants, and the puma and condor heads which are common in Tiahuanaco art, appear over a wide area of southern Peru and northern Chile, and it seems likely that for a while Tiahuanaco was the centre of a religious and political empire. We know very little about this empire, however, other than the dominance of its art style over a region.

The Tiahuanaco symbols spread much farther than the empire. They are found on pottery and statuary throughout the larger and more powerful Huari empire, whose central highland capital city of Wari, eight hundred kilometres north-west of Tiahuanaco, controlled much of highland and coastal Peru between A.D. 600 and 800. Both Tiahuanaco and Wari were apparently abandoned about the same time and Tiahuanaco religious symbols also ceased to be used over most of the empires, thus suggesting even more strongly that their original spread was for political reasons.

Tiahuanaco in its heyday was the capital of an empire and it is not surprising therefore to find some massive buildings there. They are not unusually large or unusually old; they fit within the overall pattern of Andean buildings, but, as in every other city, a few special features such as gateways and jointing methods can be found.

CENTRAL AMERICA: PALENQUE AND CHICHEN ITZA

In Central America, the jungles of Yucatan conceal some strange stone remains, most of them from the Mayan civilization, which flourished in the first thousand years A.D. The Mayan is an unusual civilization, for although it started to develop along the rivers of this area, such as the Belize, some of its major centres were in the limestone country far from rivers. These cities all relied for their water on natural storages, either swampy depressions that filled during the rainy season or nearly circular sink holes formed naturally by the collapse of large underground caverns. Limestone dissolves readily in water, so underground rivers and caves are common in this kind of country. While many caverns are dry, in some geological situations where an impervious layer such as clay is present underground lakes occur, and if the rock roof above them collapses then the water becomes available to people. Mayan settlements away from rivers are all formed round water sources of this kind.

Mayan civilization developed in a tropical forest environment where agriculture cannot be very intensive if the land is to remain fertile for long. Throughout the Mayan areas, therefore, the settlement pattern was one of small farming hamlets, each with a few families, surrounding major ceremonial centres in which few people lived but where temples, altars, shrines, sweat baths and ritual ballcourts were built. At these centres the Mayan calendars, carved on stone, were also kept. Palenque is only one of a number of ceremonial centres, of which Tikal and Copan are the most famous. All were built along similar lines, the basic plan being a rectangular plaza enclosed on three or four sides by mounds on which temples were built. The art work of the different centres varies—at Tikal relief carving is highly developed, at Bonampak wall-paintings, and at Palenque stucco sculptures—but exhibits a general similarity and a definite Mayan style.

The "Temple of Inscriptions" at Palenque is rather unusual among Mayan temples in that the mound on which it is built is hollow. Above a huge vaulted crypt at ground level rises a pyramidal platform; from this platform, 15·5 metres above the ground, sixty-five steps descend to the crypt. There is no other way in and the stair shaft was intentionally sealed with rubble in ancient times. In the crypt is a large sarcophagus with a stone slab lid, minutely carved, depicting a human being lying on a padded couch, his hands and feet bent to touch certain objects. His couch is pivoted on a maze of struts and circles, which could be an engine. In front of him looms a pointed shape with "antennae" and other objects. Surely we are dealing here with an astronaut in his rocket—an actual depiction of what some people of Palenque saw? We even know when they recorded it—in A.D. 612, according to the Mayan calendar date carved in the tomb.

If we look more closely at an actual rubbing of the

The stone with twelve corners, Cuzco, Peru

Bosses left on stones so that the Incas could lever them

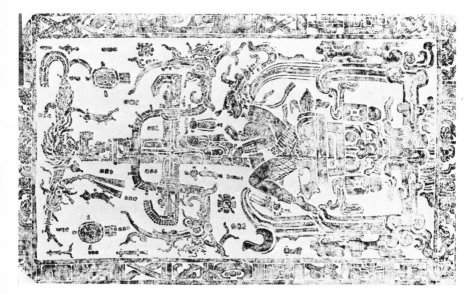

A rubbing of the whole tomb lid at Palenque

A detail of the main figure

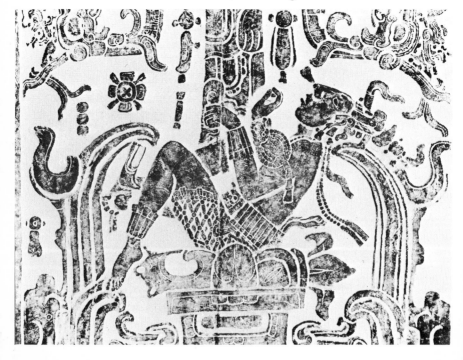

The Great Enclosure at Zimbabwe

Erecting an Easter Island statue: the actual experiment

coffin lid, however, the picture becomes less obvious. The support for the astronaut's couch is quite clearly a human skull-head and torso, with arms projecting from either side. And what is he staring so intently at and reaching for? Look at the whole structure in front of him: could it be a tree, with three branches and a fruit hanging just in front of the man? Could the creature at the top of the tree really be a bird, with its head at the left and long tail-feathers at the right. Why not?

The man is wearing a short jacket-like tunic with a broad belt and bands on his wrists and ankles. Our own spacemen certainly wear much more clothing than that, but, more importantly, this man is wearing exactly the same kind of clothing that any well-dressed Maya wore and that is displayed in hundreds of pictures and wall-paintings in every Mayan city. Sometimes lower-ranking people wore less than this—merely a loin-cloth or simple skirt—but all high-ranking people wore similar clothing. And the man who was buried in such an elaborate tomb was obviously of very high rank indeed—perhaps one of the rulers of Palenque.

When we are analysing actual objects we must believe the evidence of our eyes. We can see the skull and body on which the clearly human Maya rests, we can see the Maya is dressed like other Maya and not in a space-suit, lounge suit or jeans and T-shirt; we can see the tree with its fruit and the quetzal bird sitting above it. We can see also that this scene is repeated elsewhere in Mayan carvings, that it embodies various beliefs about the world and the after-world. And finally we might ask the question, if we are dealing with an astronaut in a rocket, how does it come to be so like our own rockets in shape and propulsion? If the earth is being regularly visited by astronauts as part of an interstellar experiment, then surely we could expect the spaceships to be rather more developed, to use an atomic or magnetic drive on their inter-galactic jaunts, to be pollution-free and computerized. Why is the Palenque astronaut using a superannuated Saturn rocket?

About A.D. 900 the Mayan civilization changed so dramatically that it is usually described as a "collapse".

Many of the ceremonial centres, with their temples and shrines, were abandoned to the jungle, and the central part of the Yucatan was almost depopulated. The reasons for this are not fully known, but a thousand years or so of intensive cultivation had probably so impoverished the soil that civilization as the Maya knew it could no longer be sustained and they moved away from some areas. In the north of Yucatan, however, where settlements began later, aspects of Mayan civilization continued for some time. Chichen Itza was one such city.

In the tenth century Chichen Itza was invaded, probably by people from the Mexican highlands called Toltecs, and they built some of the great temples and the ball-court which can be seen today. The architecture and sculpture of these temples duplicate, detail for detail, those found at Tula, the Toltec capital in Mexico.

But the Toltecs, like their Mayan predecessors, were dependent on natural wells for water. Some of these wells were so important as to be sacred, and offerings were therefore made to them. The Toltecs made many sacrifices of humans and animals and also threw in objects such as gold plaques and jade ornaments. (Jade is widely used in Central America.) Sacrifices went on until quite recently—an archaeological party investigating one of these wells even fished out a rubber doll!

The most famous *cenote*, the "Well of Sacrifice" at Chichen Itza, contained over fifty bodies and many pots, gold ornaments and other objects in the metres of thick mud at the bottom of the lake. The *cenote* itself is widely believed to be perfectly round, the relic of a rocket blast-off, and the human sacrifices to have been only of lovely young virgins, thrown in to honour the memory of the gods who left on a thunder-cloud. What are the facts?

The Well of Sacrifice is not round but oval, measuring about fifty metres north to south and about seventy metres east to west. The walls are nearly vertical, but at some places they overhang and at others are slightly cut back, though nowhere enough to allow direct access to the water. The variations in the walls can be directly related to the hardness of the different bands of limestone. The water is about ten metres deep, deepest in the centre of the *cenote*.

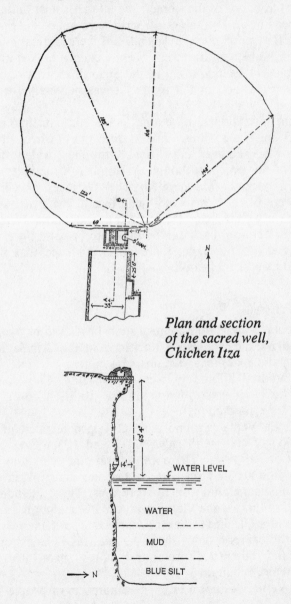

*Plan and section
of the sacred well,
Chichen Itza*

Of the fifty bodies taken out of the Chichen Itza well, some were of adult males and a high proportion were children. At least one of the women had a broken nose and others had been bashed on the skull: most were not of the *Playboy* physical type of popular legend, but were ordinary Indian women. Whether they were virgins cannot be determined with present techniques, and the Spanish records reporting the sacrifices do not tell us that it was necessary for them to be so.

Human sacrifices, of course, were common in Central American civilizations. The Aztec altars where human hearts were removed are probably the most widely known relics of this practice, though the number of sacrifices made there is usually exaggerated. The sacrifices at Chichen Itza were of the same kind—offerings to the gods, who in this case would keep the well full and allow society to survive. The well itself can be shown to be naturally formed and irregular in shape; there is no evidence that it was caused by rocket blast-off.

## CENTRAL AMERICA: LA VENTA

La Venta, with its four colossal stone heads and its pyramid-shaped mound, stands on an island in the Tonala River, among the mangrove swamps of southern Mexico, about four hundred kilometres west of Yucatan. The island is some three kilometres long, but the site itself covers only about nine hundred metres.

The La Venta pyramid is a flat-topped rectangular construction of clay, with sides of 72 and 125 metres and a height of 33 metres. There are several other clay and mud-brick mounds and terraces at the site, as well as stone monuments weighing up to forty tons. These include flat-topped altars, stone slabs with ornate sculpture on one face and stone heads two to two and a half metres high. Nine radiocarbon dates show the site was built about 800 B.C. and fell into disuse four hundred years later, after three major rebuildings.

La Venta was not a city where numbers of people lived.

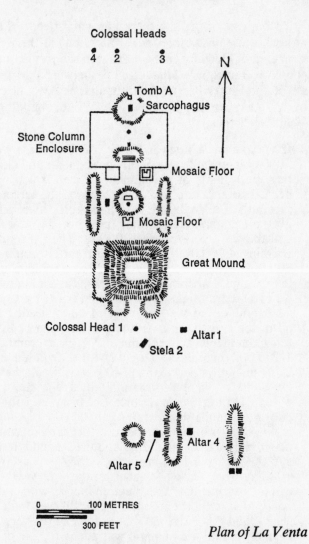

Plan of La Venta

No major occupation debris has been discovered there, while studies of the modern occupants, who use the same slash-and-burn agricultural techniques as the La Venta builders, show that not more than a hundred and fifty people could live there. Then who built it and maintained it?

I

To the east of the site there is a vast stretch of swampy ground, quite unsuitable for farming, but to the west there is an area of low hilly country that can support about twenty people to the square kilometre: perhaps 18,000 people in all. R. F. Heizer has worked out that this would certainly be an adequate population to do all the building at La Venta. He writes:

If we assume a nuclear family of five, there would be 3600 able-bodied male family heads. Careful calculations have been made of the number of men which would be needed to excavate and refill each of the large offering pits in the La Venta site, and these run between 120 and 300, on the assumption that the work day was 8 hours and the work period was 100 days. The pyramid, which contains 4,700,000 cubic feet of earth, would require 800,000 man-days to construct. Extrapolating from the few examples where we have some basis for believing that we can secure time and labor figures of the proper order of magnitude, to the man-days of labor needed to build all of the constructions in the site and import the stones for monuments and columns, we get a grand total of 1,100,000 man-days. To satisfy this requirement, only *2750* man-days per year for 400 years would be needed, but archaeological information tells us that the work was not carried out by yearly bits, but in at least four major efforts. Since the dry season of about 100 days maximum is the only convenient period for such earth-moving activity, the total man-days required would have been 275,000 per year for four years, or *687·5* per day for the 100-day work period for each of the four years. But we cannot assume that the great pyramid, with a mass of nearly five million cubic feet of earth, was built in four stages, and it is proposed that at the end of every 50-year calendar round the pyramid was added to, and that every 100 years the other mound constructions to the north of the pyramid were rebuilt.

Let us therefore separate the construction of the pyramid from the rebuildings of the mounds and ceremonial court or plaza to the north. When we do this, we note that the pyramid, which requires, in round numbers, 800,000 man-days of labor, could be built in eight 100-

day work periods. The labor requirement for each of the eight work periods is 100,000 man-days, or 1000 men working for 100 days. The mound rebuildings and court refurbishing, plus procurement of the stones for the monuments, come to an estimated 300,000 man-days. With a 100-year cycle, four work periods of 100 days each would require 75,000 man-days per *work period* or 750 men for 100 days. Thus, every 50 years 1000 men would be put to work on the pyramid, and every 100 years the work crew would expand to a total of 1750 to work on the pyramid and the mounds and court area to the north, a number which comes to only one-half of our estimated available labor force of 3600 family heads. If the period of labor service was fixed at two 20-day months, two work gangs of *1094* men, each devoting two months of 20 days to the service of the gods, could have done the job.

While these figures are crude estimates, they are none-theless based in each case upon how much earth a man can dig and carry, and upon time-reckoning periods which we have reason to believe the Olmecs knew and upon which they conducted their affairs. In other words, while I do not believe the figures are accurate in that this is how the Olmec of 2500 years ago actually planned their work, nevertheless it is reasonable to believe that this is how they may have done it. And even more to the point of the present problem, if the Olmec of this ancient date had practised slash-and-burn maize agricul-ture, they would have possessed the free time and economic surplus to carry out the work which I have outlined above. [*my alterations in italics*—P.W.]

What of the stone heads and other stones? All the stone used is volcanic and comes from quarries about a hundred kilometres to the north, up the Gulf of Mexico. We know that at this time there was already sea voyaging within the Gulf: what could be simpler than to raft the required stones down the sea-coast and then up-river? This would certainly have taken some effort, but La Venta is on a river near the coast and the quarries are close to another one, which also flows into the Gulf, so that the amount of overland transport would be minimal. And the people of La Venta did not use great quantities of stone—it was clearly a relatively scarce resource, used for special aspects of their ceremonial centre.

From La Venta also, as well as from other sites in the region, come many jade carvings. They are in styles similar to clay figurines found in large numbers throughout Central America; the jade they are made of does not come from China but is found in many parts of Central America, though not in great quantity.

The La Venta site, a semi-isolated religious centre, is similar to many other sites in Central America, for example, those of the Maya. Close to La Venta, and of the same period (about 800-400 B.C.), are Tres Zapotes and San Lorenzo, where colossal stone heads have also been found. Each place was built and maintained by a local population for their gods and attendant priests.

## AFRICA: ZIMBABWE

The great granite ruins of Zimbabwe lie in Southern Rhodesia, almost 640 kilometres from the sea. Since their discovery by Europeans just a hundred years ago they have been one of Africa's mysteries. Early explorers found quantities of golden objects in the graves there, while the circular walls of granite blocks reveal building techniques unlike those in other parts of Africa. What are these ruins and who built them? How old are they?

There are three parts to Zimbabwe—the fortified granite hill, or "Acropolis", below which lies the Great Enclosure with its high encircling wall and enigmatic tower, while scattered round the plain there is a series of other ruins similar to, but less complete than, the Great Enclosure.

The "Acropolis" or hilltop is a natural hill partly covered with enormous boulders linked together by stone walls and passages. Ascent is difficult up the steep rock-cut stairways, and the whole hilltop was strongly fortified. Large masses of occupation debris—broken pots, animal bones, walls of mud huts—occur within the walled areas on the hill and many radiocarbon dates give a consistent picture of occupation there over the last two thousand years, with most of it occurring after A.D. 1000.

As well as the surrounding wall and the solid tower, the Great Enclosure also contains other curved stone walls and a complete semi-circular enclosure of stone within the outer wall. The whole area within the main wall is covered to a depth of several metres with occupation debris and the remains of mud-hut walls. Radiocarbon dates show that occupation of the Great Enclosure started about A.D. 1400 and the style of walling used is like *some* of that found in the "Acropolis". We know that the walls and buildings were made by the people who occupied Zimbabwe at this time because in many cases older debris has been used as a foundation for some of the walls and stonework. There are also pieces of wood, especially door lintels, incorporated in some of the buildings, and these have been radiocarbon dated, giving results consistent with those of the occupation of huts within the walls.

All the walls at Zimbabwe are built of undressed, roughly rectangular, granite blocks. In the earlier walls on the hill these blocks are not laid in even courses, like bricks, but a number of blocks of different sizes are used. Later walls—sometimes built on top of or around earlier ones—are built of much more regular blocks, laid more like our bricks.

These blocks are all quite small; there are no massive stones anywhere in the Zimbabwe ruins. They are all of local granite which splits naturally into layers between three and seven inches thick. This splitting can be speeded up if a fire is lit on top of the rock and then water is thrown on the hot rock. This was done experimentally in 1961 and a large number of brick-like blocks just like those in the Zimbabwe walls were produced.

The Zimbabwe buildings contain a great many of these stone blocks, even through in all the walls they are used only as facings, the wall cores being simply rubble. The main encircling wall of the Great Enclosure is 240 metres long and has a maximum height of ten metres. It is up to five metres thick at the base but narrows towards the top.

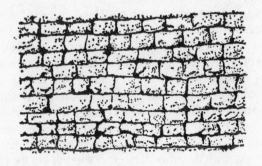

*Wall-building techniques at Zimbabwe*

This technique was necessary because the builders used no mortar at all in the construction and it was much safer and stronger to taper a dry-stone wall towards the top.

That the Zimbabwe builders were not specially skilled is clear from a number of things. None of the walls are straight or even; when two walls meet they are not linked together with interleaving blocks but stand flush, one against the other; foundations are very rare and quite often walls have been simply built on the roughly levelled ground surface. In other words, as stone-workers the Zimbabwe builders were only second-rate.

But there is one enigma at Zimbabwe—the conical tower within the Great Enclosure. This tower is made of granite blocks, it is solid—there is no chamber within it—and it is at least 10·5 metres high. Was it a watchtower, or a place for religious ceremonies? We do not know. But we do know that it was built within the Great Enclosure where several score people lived. The pattern of their living arrangements is entirely African—the layout of houses, walls and storage areas is duplicated in many other situations. Even the ground plan of the palace of the Paramount chief of Barotseland, still in use in the 1950s, looks like that of Zimbabwe, as do many other African dwelling enclosures.

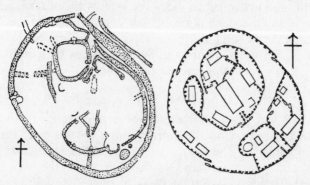

*Ground plans of the Great Enclosure at Zimbabwe* (left), *and the palace of the Paramount Chief of Barotseland* (right)

Zimbabwe, of course, is not unique. There are over three hundred other ruins built of stone in Southern Rhodesia—forts, terraces, walls and stone-lined pits are found in many parts of the country. None of these are as complex or as striking as Zimbabwe, but they are built with similar techniques and according to similar patterns—techniques and patterns that appear to be indigenous and certainly show few similarities to stone constructions in other parts of the world.

Zimbabwe may well have become important for a number

of reasons. The small region surrounding it is a particularly
favoured one and, owing to the rains and mists that sweep
up the Mtelikwi valley from the Indian Ocean throughout
the year, it is an oasis of greenery in a dry area of country.
The granite hill on which the "Acropolis" was built dominates this area and would thus be selected as a base by
people living there. There is evidence from the burials with
golden objects that a religious cult was practised on the hill,
and this has nothing to do with gods from the sky, but
rather with ancestors and attempts to maintain the special
status of Zimbabwe.

In spite of many theories, including those that have seen
Zimbabwe as symbolizing a foetus in a human uterus or a
giant sundial, nothing non-African or out of place has ever
been found in the ruins. They are built with local materials
in a distinctive technique, which can be seen to become
more accurate and more finished in appearance as time
goes on. In other words, the builders learnt by experience,
their knowledge was not imposed from outside.

### SOUTH-WEST ASIA: BAALBEK

Baalbek is a city in Lebanon, whose importance in ancient
times centred round the worship of a special god, Jupiter
Heliopolitanus. The Romans conquered the area about two
thousand years ago and established there the city they
called Heliopolis—Sun City—to relate it both to the
emperor and to the sun-god, Jupiter. Roman imperial money
was used to build an immense temple which sits on a platform of large stone blocks. Three of these blocks in the
western wall of the terrace weigh 750 tons each. They are
19·5 metres long, 4·5 metres wide and 3.75 metres thick.
But there are only three of them—a fourth lies abandoned
in a local quarry where all the stone was cut and dressed.
It is clear that the three giant blocks were the first to be cut
and used as foundations, but then even the Romans found
the task was not worth the effort, and all later blocks
weigh a mere 250 tons and are only nine metres long.
These blocks were used to build all the rest of the temple
foundations.

There is no evidence of a pre-Roman settlement at Baalbek, though the name suggests that this existed. But all the buildings there today have been constructed with Roman techniques and styles, while the colossal size of the temples and blocks is repeated in other cities built by the empire of Rome.

STRANGE BUILDINGS OR CITIES OF MEN?

All over the world, in America, Africa, and Asia, men have made buildings—palaces, temples, houses—of stone. Sometimes they have used stone from far-away places cut into unexpected shapes for their works, but generally they have used conveniently available local stone, broken or cut into simple, squared-off blocks. In each area the building techniques differ, but within each there is clear evidence of tradition and continuity.

If mankind was taught by beings from other worlds to make stone buildings, why should they be so different in different parts of the world? If astronauts themselves carved and moved giant stones, why are so many different styles and techniques used? And why should astronauts construct stone buildings anyway? *Our* space travellers take their own equipment with them and erect portable dwellings within a few minutes; they take their own food, their own local transport. Is it logical to interpret buildings which are *not* unique and do *not* require superhuman powers to build as the creation of outside forces? None of them *could* not have been built by men; nothing extra-terrestrial has ever been found within any of them. Each building, palace, temple and city was built by men in honour of their gods, kings, and themselves. We build skyscrapers, cathedrals, and opera houses, sometimes with vast expenditure of money and effort. Should we deny that our ancestors could do the same, each people in its own way?

# 8. The Navel of the World

Easter Island is a tiny speck of land 22 kilometres long and 11 kilometres wide, at the eastern end of Polynesia, 1,450 kilometres from any other island and 3,700 kilometres from the coast of Chile. It is best known for its giant statues, more than six hundred at the last count, which range in weight from about five tons to 130 tons for the largest, which was never finished. Who made these statues? How were they cut out of the rock and moved across the island? What were they for?

Easter Island is formed by an enormous extinct volcano, and at least five craters can still be seen around the island. All the statues on the island were carved on the southern slopes of one crater, called Rano Raraku. Both the inner and outer slopes of the crater were used because the rock of this area was the easiest to carve. At least eighteen different quarry areas can be seen and tens of thousands of cubic metres of rock have been removed. As one visitor said, "It is impossible today to visualize how the volcano looked originally. The quarrying activity and the enormous quantity of rubble have completely altered the local topography."

Rano Raraku crater is of yellowish volcanic tuff, a rock formed of compressed ash. It is not much harder than chalk, except when it is exposed to the weather. It then becomes steel hard, a phenomenon found in many types of stone and known as "case-hardening". As one of the Spaniards who landed on the island wrote, "having tried it myself with an [iron] hoe, it struck fire: a proof of its density." But underneath the hard exterior the rock is softer and can be cut and shaped quite easily with stone tools. How do we know this?

In 1956 Thor Heyerdahl—the man responsible for the Kon-Tiki raft voyage from America to the Pacific Islands—led an expedition to investigate many aspects of Easter Island's past. In the quarries of Rano Raraku he found thousands of pointed stone picks lying round the 166 unfinished statues. He therefore decided to experiment.

Could these simple stone picks, which seemed to be made to fit into human hands, really be the tools used to cut and shape the giant statues? He discussed this with the islanders, descendants of the original inhabitants, and they insisted that these were what their forefathers had used. So one morning he hired six men to start once again the work that had been stopped so many years ago.

The leader of the men measured out a statue's proportions in arm and hand lengths and the six started bashing away with their hand-held picks. Each blow raised only a small patch of dust. The workmen frequently splashed the rock with water in order to make it softer. The stone picks soon became blunt and were changed for fresh ones, until after a time all had been used. They were then re-sharpened by chipping off a series of small flakes round the point, just as if a pencil was being sharpened.

After three days the outline of a statue was visible and Heyerdahl had some idea of the rate of work. The statue being made was about five metres long, not a very large one by Easter Island standards. The islanders, Heyerdahl, and another archaeologist all calculated how long it would take to finish. Each of them concluded that six men, working every day, could complete it in twelve to fifteen months.

Was there time for the Easter Islanders to have made all the statues on the island? No exact listing has ever been made of the number of statues, but a rough count gives between six and seven hundred, with perhaps two hundred more partly made, unfinished and broken ones still in the quarries and buried under the rubble piles. Many of the finished statues are five to ten metres tall—certainly larger than the experimental one—and more than six workmen would probably have been needed to finish one of these within a year. But certainly twenty workmen, in two teams of ten men, could finish any one of the statues in a year.

All the statues on Easter Island could have been made by twenty-man teams working continuously for eight hundred years. Was Easter Island settled for as long as this?

As well as experimenting with statues, Heyerdahl's expedition also excavated a number of archaeological sites and collected charcoal for radiocarbon-14 dating. Two of the dates they obtained show that there were men on Easter Island before A.D. 500.

At the other end of the time scale we know that the statues were all toppled over during intertribal wars about A.D. 1700. The first European to visit Easter Island, Jacob Roggeven, saw some statues still standing in 1722, but it is likely that statue carving ceased at some time in that period.

In the 1,200 years from 500 to 1700 there was clearly enough time for all the statues to be made, even if only one statue was carved a year—and we have no proof that the Easter Islanders limited themselves to this.

Once the statues were carved in the quarries of Rano Raraku, they had to be moved. More than three hundred statues were transported from the quarry area, some of them as far as ten kilometres, a major journey for a monolith weighing fifty tons or so!

Easter Island traditions say that the statues walked by themselves under the influence of charms or supernatural powers possessed only by chiefs and priests. Walking statues must have been an unusual sight, especially since none of the traditionally shaped ones have legs; they consist of head, arms and torso only. Only one statue has legs, and this is a unique figure found by Heyerdahl's expedition. It was in such poor condition that it had not formerly been recognized as a statue, even by the Easter Islanders. But if the statues did not walk, how did they move?

The statues that were moved across the island generally

seem to have weighed between twelve and twenty-five tons, but some much larger ones, weighing about eighty tons, were also transported. This was certainly a major task, but once again the modern islanders had some very practical ideas on the subject. They knew the legends, but they also knew that statues did not walk by themselves. They knew that there was not enough wood on the island for rollers. But there *was* enough wood to make sledges. Once again Heyerdahl conducted an experiment.

The Easter Islanders made a wooden sledge and attached it to a statue weighing about ten tons. Ropes made from tree bark were attached to the sledge and then invitations were sent out for everyone to come to a feast. About one hundred and fifty people—men, women and children—turned up to eat, drink, dance, and finally to pull. And pull they did until the statue on its sledge slid away over the plain. More people and greater care would be required when larger statues were to be moved. But if 150 people can move a 10-ton statue, 1,500 people can move a 100-ton statue. The pre-European population of Easter Island numbered between 2,000 and 4,000 people—no one disputes that—and most of these people would be available to help move the occasional giant statue.

Theorists have suggested other ways of moving the Easter Island statues. One of the more ingenious ideas relies on the fact that some statue bases are curved and flared in a special way so that if the statue were stood upright the base of the torso could be used as a point of balance. Using a wooden sheer-legs and ropes the statue could be rocked forwards and backwards until it "walked" along between its sheer-legs.* Far fewer people would be required if this method was used and there would also be much less friction between the figure and the ground. This, of course, may be the origin of the legends that the statues "walked" from the quarry to the temples where they were erected.

* For a fuller account see Heyerdahl, *Reports of the Norwegian Archaeological Expedition to Easter Island and the East Pacific*, vol. 1, p. 371.

Prayers and chants would be added to ensure that the ropes did not break and the statues fall over.

How were the statues, weighing between ten and eighty tons, stood upright, not merely in holes in the ground—as some of them were—but also on specific points on temple platforms? Once again, many theories have been proposed, but the one the Easter Islanders themselves suggested seems as good as any and worked perfectly when tried. The tools used were two long poles, some ropes and a pile of stones. The statue chosen for the experiment was a large one, three metres wide across the shoulders and weighing about twenty-five tons. It lay three metres below the level of the platform on which it had stood hundreds of years ago, so that it had to be raised vertically as well as stood upright.

Twelve men, six a side, took the poles and began levering under the statue. Each time they moved the mono-lith a fraction other men quickly inserted small stones under it so that the advance was a permanent one. After ten days the statue was raised on a pile of stones level with the plat-form on which it was to stand. Then the levers went to work under the head. Gradually the head was raised until the figure rose to an angle of about forty-five degrees to the horizontal. Because the levers were now too far above the ground to be reached directly, ropes were tied to them and the men stood below pulling on them. Ropes were also attached to the statue's neck and anchored out at the front, back and sides so that it would not topple over. A little more, very careful levering and the statue slid forward, rocked, and stood upright on its platform. Twelve men, two poles, eighteen days, to raise a 25-ton statue. Who needs astronauts?

The statues, of course, were only one part of a more complex image, for in earlier times each body had a bright-red stone hat or topknot balanced on its head. These cylindrical topknots, which weighed anything up to thirty tons, were carved from soft volcanic scoria at another vol-canic crater twelve kilometres from the statue's quarry. From Puna Pau quarry they were moved to the statues and balanced on their heads. To the Easter Islanders, who wer' used to moving stone giants, the transport of these topknots must have been easy, and it is not difficult to decide how they were placed on the statues' heads.

Once the statue itself had been stood upright, there was still a large pile of stones in front of it, reaching up to its chin. The red topknot was moved up this pile by the same simple set of ropes and wooden levers. It was then slid sideways on to the statue's head, where it was carefully balanced. That being done, the pile of stones could be taken away, leaving the statue with its red topknot to baffle all those who underestimate human muscle power and primitive people's ingenuity.

As well as the statues, Easter Island is famous for three other mysteries: fine masonry walls that look like some found in South America, pictures and legends of "birdmen", and wooden tablets covered with lines of small pictures, often said to be writing but as yet unread by anyone.

Do these things demonstrate long-ago connections with lost civilizations, with South America and with visitors from outer space? Or were they perhaps the invention of a group of people who, living for hundreds of years in the total isolation of Easter Island, developed and modified the way of life that they had brought with them? Who are the Easter Islanders anyway?

There are many legends about the origins of Pacific peoples, not the least colourful being some invented by people who have never been there. They include ideas of lost and sunken continents, lost tribes of Israel, migrations from India, China, North America or Peru. None of these is true.

Easter Island itself is a giant extinct volcano that thrusts up from the flat ocean floor of the eastern Pacific Ocean. It is highly magnetic, as are all volcanic islands. It is not the drowned remains of an extinct continent; all geologists are agreed that the Pacific Ocean floor, now mapped as well as most parts of the globe, shows no signs of any continental remains less than tens or perhaps hundreds of millions of years old. Sediments taken from the ocean floor by the Swedish Deep Sea Expedition in 1949 show that their slow accumulation has remained undisturbed for at least one million years.

There are no signs of a vanished civilization on Easter Island either. If there was ever an advanced civilization in the Pacific, surely it would leave more visible traces than a few stone statues and some carved wooden tablets? Where are the roads, the houses, the metal, china and glass utensils? Civilizations leave remains; so far we have none in the Pacific.

The facts of Pacific settlement are more straightforward. We may start with language. The Easter Island language is Polynesian, like all the languages spoken in the giant triangle of Polynesia, stretching from Hawaii to New Zealand and to Easter Island itself. Polynesian languages are mutually intelligible, like English, American and Australian, which shows that the various islanders have not been isolated on their islands for more than a couple of thousand years.

All Polynesian languages are but one branch of an enormously widespread language family called Austronesian. Austronesian languages are found on most Pacific islands, in Indonesia and south-east Asia, and on Madagascar. None are found in the Americas or India or China.

So the language evidence suggests strongly that the original settlers of the Pacific came from south-east Asia. This is confirmed by the archaeological evidence. The first Pacific islands to be settled were New Guinea and Australia, more than thirty thousand years ago, and man only gradually moved eastwards from there. The first men came to Fiji about four thousand years ago, according to the radio-carbon dates. These people were good sailors, able to make direct voyages between islands three or four hundred kilometres apart. They were also farmers, growing such crops as taro, breadfruit, bananas and sugar-cane, and keeping pigs, dog and fowls. All these crops and animals are south-east Asian in origin; with the exception of dogs, they were all unknown in the Americas until introduced by Europeans. Their tools, weapons and ornaments were common throughout the Pacific islands—simple ground-stone axes, arm-rings made of polished pieces of shell, various kinds of nets and hooks for fishing.

It was from the island areas of the central Pacific—Fiji, Tonga, and above all Samoa—that people colonized Polynesia. In the one or more thousand years that it took to settle the Polynesian islands, the Polynesians certainly developed aspects of their culture in ways unlike those found in other parts of the Pacific. They stopped making pottery and relied on pit-cooking; they developed double-outrigger canoes, making them much more stable for sea voyaging; they developed and expanded the idea of the assembly court for village meetings until the *marae* became a central feature of Polynesian life. As they moved into and lived in Polynesia they became the Polynesians we know today, outstandingly successful in their island environment.

The Easter Islanders are Polynesians. Where do the statues, the masonry, and the "written" tablets fit in?

Precise information about why the Easter Islanders erected the giant statues can no longer be obtained. The last statues were set in place at least three hundred years ago and traditional religious beliefs have been crushed by Christian missionaries. The Dutch explorers in 1722 said: "We noticed only that they kindle fires in front of certain remarkably tall stone figures they set up; and, thereafter squatting on their heels with heads bowed down, they bring the palms of their hands together and alternately raise and lower them."

Captain James Cook, who visited the island in 1774, decided the statues "are not, in my opinion, looked upon as idols by the present inhabitants. . . . On the contrary, I rather suppose that they are burying places for certain tribes or families." The scientist Forster, who was with Cook, actually asked the islanders what the statues were for and "concluded that they were monuments erected to the memory of some of their areekees, or kings".

By 1866, when French missionaries settled permanently on Easter Island, most of the statues had been overthrown in island wars and, in addition, nearly all of the people had been taken as slaves to Peruvian mines in 1864. Very few

K

of them ever returned and most of the traditional knowledge was lost. Information collected since that time tends
to confirm Cook's opinion that the statues were a kind of
monument, but it is also likely that the spirits of the chiefs
thus commemorated had joined the islanders' gods and
could be called on to assist in worldly affairs.

Large stone statues in human form occur in other islands
of south-eastern Polynesia as well as on Easter Island,
although the classic, severe, long-faced Easter Island form
is only found there. And the classic form is not the only
kind of statue to be found on Easter Island. In 1956 Heyerdahl's expedition found a number of other statues, some
with round heads and small ears, others with almond-shaped
eyes and one with a small goatee beard. Some of these
statues, which belong archaeologically to the Early Period,
look like those found on other Polynesian islands, and they
are also similar to wooden carvings of human form which
are quite common throughout the whole of Polynesia. In
other words, the Easter Island statues are not a unique
occurrence. What *is* unique is their uniformity, their size
and their number. But these things are explicable if we
realize that Easter Island was settled by one group of people
who remained there, in isolation, for more than a thousand
years. What they did was develop one particular cultural
form to extremes. They might have done this with dancing,
oratory or wood-carving, but since they came from islands
where stone-carving was practised to an island with an
abundance of good stone to carve, it is not very surprising
that statues became their ruling passion. Motor cars are
their equivalent in Australia. The particular form of statue
the Easter Islanders finally settled on is more of a mystery.
There is nothing much like it elsewhere in Polynesia, or in
South America; there is no obvious model for it. The earliest
statues on the island are more like those found elsewhere
in Polynesia, so perhaps the classic Easter Island statues
were something the islanders themselves developed, in
isolation from the world. There are, certainly, some hints of
the later form in the early statues of the island, but precisely
how that form developed we do not know.

Many of the statues were erected on special bases inside stone structures called *ahu*. *Ahu* are the island's common ceremonial buildings. They consist of a rectangular platform built of earth, stones and rubble, with ramps up to the platform at either end. That, at least, is the basic form, though many minor variations can be found among the 244 known *ahu* on the island. Some are small cairns rather than platforms, some were made for statues to be erected on, others were simply irregular mounds of stones. But they had one feature in common—all were burial places, with human bones being deposited in these mausoleums.

About one half of the *ahu* were designed to have statues erected on them, and they were therefore built with carefully prepared bases on the platforms, which stood two to three metres above the surrounding country. To take the weight of the statues, the back wall of the platform usually consisted of large blocks of stone which acted as a retaining wall. In a few instances these large stones have been carefully shaped and ground so that they fit together precisely. The masonry walls they form are very like some of those found in South America, especially around Tiahuanaco. Are they really part of the same tradition? Let us look at a few facts.

We have already seen that stone-working was common in south-east Polynesia. On other islands in the same region fortified hilltop villages were built, using very similar stone-working techniques. Dry-stone walling and other uses of stone are common even farther west, in Tahiti, Hawaii, Tonga and Fiji. In other words, Easter Island is not alone in the Pacific: it is part of a culture with a tradition of stone-working.

On the other hand, the techniques that are used in wall-building on Easter Island and in South America are quite different. The walls at Tiahuanaco are solid stone structures, made simply of fitted blocks; the Easter Island walls were a retaining façade; behind them the platforms were built up of irregular stones, earth and rubble. This technique was the normal one in the other Pacific islands.

Finally, if the techniques of fine masonry were derived

from South America, we should expect them to occur early in the island's history. The first men who came from across the sea or through the air would remember best, and attempt to copy as well as they could, the methods they had used at home. As the years went by they might lose some of the art, change it and modify it. But this is not what happened.

Although not enough careful archaeological work has been done on Easter Island for every detail to be clear, it is fairly certain that the finely made masonry façades and most of the classic statues were created in what is known as the Middle Period. This period has been dated by radiocarbon-14 dating to A.D. 1200 and later—that is, hundreds of years after the first settlement of the island. The most famous *ahu*, known as Vinapu 1, which has the finest and most complex basalt-block retaining wall, certainly dates from this time. So that the masonry techniques, like the statues themselves, were the Easter Islanders' own development of a tradition that already existed in Polynesia.

What about the *ahu* themselves?

*Ahu*, mausoleums for the chiefs of large family groupings, are very similar to those in ceremonial structures found throughout Polynesia. These structures, called *marae*, are a rectangular court with a low platform, called *ahu*, along the back wall. The platform is often marked by several upright stone slabs and is a sacred area. The court is usually a meeting place for the villagers. One of the striking facts about the Easter Island *ahu* is that some of them have courtyards marked out by walls while others at least have a piece of levelled ground where a courtyard would be expected. And it is the earliest *ahu* in Easter Island's history that are most like those in Polynesian *marae* in having the best developed courtyards.

We may therefore summarize this section by saying that the finest masonry, *ahu* and statues all developed locally on Easter Island.

Easter Island's greatest single religious festival was that of the bird-man. This was an annual ceremony that gave rise to many violent passions and also to many carvings on boulders on one part of Easter Island. There are at least 150 representations of the bird-man symbol, very often with an egg in his hand, as well as many carvings of birds, faces, boats, dance paddles, and other objects.

The basis of the cult was to find the first egg of the year laid by a sooty tern on the tiny off-shore island of Moto-nui. The egg was the incarnation of the god Makemake, and the chief who found this egg gained divine favour as well as a number of earthly benefits. To gain the prize required physical courage—a swim across the shark-filled sea to the islet, and then a long wait, constantly on the lookout for the elusive brown speckled egg.

The god Makemake was the islanders' supreme deity, responsible for the creation of the earth, heavenly bodies and man himself. But he acted together with another god, Haua, in bringing the birds and the bird-cult to the island. Interestingly it is Makemake who is portrayed as a human while Haua is part bird, part man.

The cult of the bird-man is dated first at around A.D. 1000-1200 by similarities between the masonry techniques of various cult houses and the *ahu*. Since all traces of the cult have been proscribed by Christian missionaries for over a century, it is difficult to find out many details about it, but we can estimate that its fully developed form occurred only in the Middle Period and later.

Even early Europeans were seen as sources of power and influence, possible helpers in the annual search. Evidence for this is seen in the paintings of three-masted ships on the walls of small stone houses near the site of the ceremony. Neither Easter Islanders nor South Americans had such ships. We may also note that no paintings of flying saucers or other space-craft appear in the records.

According to islanders in the nineteenth century, those who sought the help of the gods did so in the form of set prayers, usually in chanting form. These chants were known only to a group of priests who, while singing them, held small wooden tablets carved with lines of small figures such as human beings, fish, birds, plants and geometric designs. All figures are the same size, all are stylized, all are in lines.

The *rongorongo* tablets were first recorded in the 1860s by missionaries, who noted that every house had some of them. Could they be writing, records in some strange old script?

The first missionaries to the island certainly thought so, and Father Zumbohm in about 1868 attempted to find out more about the mysterious tablets. His own words tell the story:

> I gathered together the most learned of our Indians to interrogate them on the meaning of these characters, which had every appearance of a hieroglyphic script. All appeared to be content to see this object [the wooden tablet] and they told me its name which I have forgotten, whereupon some of them started to read the text by singing. But others shouted: "No it is not like that!" The disagreement among my teachers was so great that, in spite of my effort, I was not much more informed after their lesson than beforehand.

Later investigators fared no better. No Easter Islander has ever been found who could either identify the meaning of individual signs or groups of signs or who could repeat with any consistency at different times any text said to be associated with the tablets.

Today there are only twenty-six known pieces of wood with the lines of carving on them. Most of them come from Easter Island, but one is a European oar-blade and must therefore date from the seventeenth century or later. The tablets are now scattered through the world's museums.

Attempts to decipher the carving on the Easter Island tablets have been made by many linguists and at least one trained cryptographer. They have established that groups of signs are repeated on various tablets and also that a very few symbols occur with great frequency—on one tablet, for instance, the image of the sooty tern occurs once in every five symbols. If each symbol is a word or phrase then this was an extremely repetitive language.

At present there are two ways to approach the problem. One is to assume that the Easter Island tablets record a totally foreign and unknown language, a language which no Easter Islander knew how to speak or translate, but which they continued to carve on wooden boards, and sing chants in. This language used as symbols the everyday objects found on Easter Island. Unlike most languages, it did not use any conventional signs, and its symbols were not completely uniform. For example, human figures show different position of heads, legs and arms, and no one has so far been able to show that these occur with a regularity that might denote changes of meaning.

There are other problems, too. Whatever the size and shape of the wooden tablet, it is invariably covered with signs on both sides and even along the edges. Not the slightest space is wasted on any of the tablets, which occur in chance shapes—an oar-blade, for instance. If the signs corresponded to texts, or prayers, or chants, was each exactly the length to fit on a piece of wood? If even several texts were inscribed on each piece of wood, did they all fit exactly? And why were they not separated by a space or conventional sign, like a stroke or a full stop?

The other approach to the problem is to look for a link between chants and tablets in the context of the Polynesian society that existed on Easter Island. The idea of a special group of priests who knew the chanting prayers by heart, as well as genealogies and legends, is a common one in Polynesia. In many other islands—New Zealand, Tahiti, the Marquesas—these bards carried some finely made emblem which they flourished while chanting. This was not a text or even a series of notes, since they knew the chants by heart; rather the emblem was to emphasize to the listeners what the bard was saying. We might make a comparison with many Christian priests, who know the prayers off by heart, but still use a prayer book as a concrete reminder to themselves and the congregation of the prayers that they are saying.

The emblems used in Polynesia varied from place to place. The Maori orators in New Zealand used a finely engraved club, those in Tahiti a carved staff, while the Marquesan bards flourished bags of coconut fibre from which hung knotted cords. In each case the objects were carefully made and used materials and decorative motifs common in other aspects of their island's culture.

The comparison with Easter Island is clear. All the islanders agreed that the tablets and chants were related in some way, while the symbols carved on the tablets are similar to many carved on rocks in the area of the island where the bird-man cult was practised. So it seems very likely that these carved tablets were simply symbolic representations of chants. They were not carved with a language of words or even clauses in a particular chant, but were decorated with magical symbols specifically chosen by the priest who made the tablet. To him, and him alone, they may have constituted some kind of a reminder of his chants, but no one else would be able to "translate" the tablet.

It is now time to draw together the various parts of the history of Easter Island.

The tiny volcanic speck was first settled by humans less than two thousand years ago. The people who found this lonely outpost were Polynesians, part of the group of sea-going agricultural peoples who settled the great triangle of Polynesia between 1000 B.C. and A.D. 1000. The early Easter Islanders brought with them the knowledge of stone-tool making, the crops sweet potato, sugar-cane and bananas, and the domestic fowl. The fact that many plants, as well as the domestic dog and pig, widely known in Polynesia, were missing from the Easter Island ceremony in 1722 suggests that the settlement of the island was a once-only affair and that there was no subsequent contact across the two thousand kilometres of ocean separating it from the next inhabited land in any direction. The first Easter Islanders would also have come with some Polynesian religious beliefs, some practices involving masonry structures for religious, assembly and burial purposes, and some tradition of carving in wood and stone, including the engraving of naturalistic designs such as are found in many parts of Polynesia.

They arrived on an island where there were few native plants, only one species of tree and one shrub, and even fewer animals—only insects and a few birds. The island did, however, have plentiful stone which was easy to carve, as well as a vast surface litter of stone. In the near-absence of wood, the Easter Islanders became expert stone-workers. They built houses out of stone slabs, they carved statues in a locally evolved style to commemorate their dead chieftains, they chipped fine tools out of the sharp, brittle volcanic glass that was also present on the island. Not only did they carve stone, they learnt how to move it round in large pieces. Without machines, but with intelligence and muscle power, they manipulated the giant statues out of the quarry at Rano Raraku, across the island and stood them on well-made platforms. They did it in the past as they have demonstrated they can do it today.

They created their own version of Polynesian culture. Admittedly, after 1,500 years or so some aspects of it did not look very much like the cultures to be found on other Polynesian islands, but archaeology, linguistics, and physical anthropology all show that that was its source. Easter Islanders, human like ourselves, created the so-called mysteries of "the navel of the world".

L

# Further Reading

The books and articles listed below are the main sources for the statements in the book. They should also give anyone who wants to check up on me a fairly good idea of the important writings in the subject.

## CHAPTER 1

J. Deetz, *Invitation to Archaeology*. Natural History Press, New York, 1967.

D. Brothwell and E. S. Higgs (eds), *Science in Archaeology*. Thames and Hudson, London, 1971.

R. E. M. Wheeler, *Archaeology from the Earth*. Penguin, 1956.

## CHAPTER 2

C. Loring Brace, *The Stages of Human Evolution*. Prentice-Hall, Englewood Cliffs, N.J., 1967.

M. H. Day, *Fossil Man*. Hamlyn—Sun Books, 1969.

R. H. Osborne (ed.), *The Biological and Social Meaning of Race*. W. H. Freeman, San Francisco, 1971.

D. Pilbeam, *The Ascent of Man*. Macmillan, 1972.

## CHAPTER 3

J. E. Pfeiffer, *The Emergence of Man*. Nelson, London, 1969.

J. V. S. Megaw and R. Jones, *The Dawn of Man*. Wayland, London, 1972.

S. Struever (ed.), *Prehistoric Agriculture*. American Museum of Natural History Sourcebooks. 1971.

R. M. Adams, *The Evolution of Urban Society*. Weidenfeld and Nicolson, London, 1966.

E. P. Lanning, *Peru Before the Incas*. Prentice-Hall, 1967.

W. T. Sanders and B. Price, *Mesoamerica*. Random House, New York, 1968.

CHAPTER 4

I. E. S. Edwards, *The Pyramids of Egypt*. 2nd ed. Pelican, 1961.

J. Weeks, *The Pyramids*. Cambridge University Press, 1972.

A. Lucas and J. R. Harris, *Ancient Egyptian Materials and Industries*. Edward Arnold, London, 1962.

R. Engelbach, *The Problem of the Obelisks*. T. Fisher Unwin, London, 1923.

G. A. Reisner, *Mycerinus*. Harvard University Press, 1931.

W. M. Flinders Petrie, *Egyptian Architecture*. London, 1938.

*The Pyramids and Temples of Gizeh*. 2 vols. London, 1883.

CHAPTER 5

W. Arndt, "The Interpretation of the Delemere Lightning Painting and Rock Engravings", *Oceania*, 32, 1961, pp. 163-77.

I. M. Crawford, *The Art of the Wandjina*. Oxford University Press, 1968.

R. M. Berndt (ed.), *Australian Aboriginal Art*. Ure Smith, Sydney, 1964.

E. Ten Raa, "Dead Art and Living Society: A Study of Rock Paintings in a Social Context", *Mankind*, 8, 1971, pp. 42-58.

J-D. Lajoux, *The Rock Paintings of Tassili*. Thames & Hudson, London, 1962.

H. Lhote, *The Search for the Tassili Frescoes*. Hutchinson, London, 1959.

E. Anati, *Camonica Valley*. A. A. Knopf, New York, 1961.

N. K. Sandars, *Prehistoric Art in Europe*. Pelican History of Art, 1968.

## CHAPTER 6

*Nazca and Peru*

P. Kosok and M. Reiche, "The Mysterious Markings of Nazca," *Natural History*, May 1947, pp. 220-38.

P. Kosok and M. Reiche, "Ancient Drawings on the Desert of Peru", *Archaeology*, 2, 1949, pp. 206-15.

A. L. Kroeber and W. D. Strong, "The Uhle Collections from Chincha", *University of California Publications in American Archaeology and Ethnology*, 21, 1924, pp. 92-4.

E. P. Lanning, *Peru Before the Incas*. Prentice-Hall, 1967.

G. Kubler, *The Art and Architecture of Ancient America*. Pelican History of Art, 1962.

*Piri Re'is Map*

C. Hapgood, *Maps of the Ancient Sea Kings*. Chilton Books, New York, 1965.

R. A. Skelton and others, *The Vinland Map and the Tartar Relation*. Yale University Press, 1966.

J. R. Hale, *Renaissance Exploration*. B.B.C., 1968.

L. Bagrow, *History of Cartography*. Revised and enlarged by R. A. Skelton. C. A. Watts, London, 1964.

*The Maya*

M. D. Coe, *The Maya*. Pelican, 1971.

G. R. Willey, *An Introduction to American Archaeology*, vol. 1. Prentice-Hall, 1966.

J. B. de Casas, "The Mexican Calendar as compared to other Mesoamerican systems", *Acta Ethnologica et Linguistica*, No. 15. Vienna, 1969.

CHAPTER 7

G. H. S. Bushnell, *Peru*. Thames and Hudson, London, 1956.

E. P. Lanning, *Peru Before the Incas*. Prentice-Hall, 1967.

J. Steward (ed.), *Handbook of South American Indians*, vols. 2, 5. Bureau of American Ethnology, Bulletin, 143, 1963.

G. Kubler, *The Art and Architecture of Ancient America*. Pelican, 1962.

G. R. Willey, *An Introduction to American Archaeology*. 2 vols. Prentice-Hall, 1966-9.

M. D. Coe, *The Maya*. Pelican, 1971.

R. Summers, *Zimbabwe*. Nelson, London, 1963.

B. Fagan, *Southern Africa during the Iron Age*. Thames and Hudson, London, 1965.

R. F. Heizer, "Agriculture and the Theocratic State in Lowland Mexico", *American Antiquity*, 26, 1960, pp. 215-22.

R. F. Heizer, "Ancient Heavy Transport, Methods and Achievements", *Science*, 153, 1966, pp. 821-30.

CHAPTER 8

T. Heyerdahl, *Aku-aku*. G. Allen and Unwin, London, 1958.

T. Heyerdahl (ed.), *Reports of the Norwegian Archaeological Expedition to Easter Island and the East Pacific*, 2 vols. G. Allen and Unwin, 1961 and 1965.

A. Metraux, *Easter Island*. Deutsch, London, 1957.

A. Metraux, *Ethnology of Easter Island*, Bulletin of the B. P. Bishop Museum, 160, 1940.

J. Golson, "Thor Heyerdahl and the Prehistory of Easter Island", *Oceania*, 36, 1965, pp. 38-83.

R. Wauchope, *Lost Tribes and Sunken Continents*. University of Chicago Press, 1962.

R. C. Suggs, *Island Civilizations of Polynesia*. Mentor Books, New York, 1960.

L. Groube, "Tonga, Lapita Pottery and Polynesian Origins", *Journal of the Polynesian Society*, 80, 1971, pp. 278-316.

# Index